move up

Elementary
Teacher's Book

A

MACMILLAN
HEINEMANN
English Language Teaching

Simon Greenall

Macmillan Heinemann English Language Teaching, Oxford

A division of Macmillan Publishers Limited

Companies and representatives throughout the world

ISBN 0 435 29787 2

Layout by eMC Design
Cover design by Stafford & Stafford

Note to teachers
The two tests and Practice Book Answer Key at the back of
this book may be photocopied for use in class without the prior
written permission of Macmillan Publishers Limited. However,
please note that the copyright law, which dose not normally
permit multiple copying of published material, applies to the
rest of this book.

Author's Acknowledgments

I am very grateful to all the people who have contributed towards the
creation of this book. My thanks are due to:

- All the teachers I have had the privilege to meet on seminars in
  many different countries and the various people who have
  influenced my work.
- Paul Ruben for producing the tapes, and the actors for their voices.
- The various schools who piloted the material.
- Simon Stafford for his skilful design.
- James Hunter and Bridget Green for their careful attention to
  detail and their creative contribution.
- Angela Reckitt for her careful management of the project.
- Jessica Rackham for her extremely thorough and efficient
  editorial input.
- And last, but by no means least, Jill, Jack, and Alex.

Printed in Hong Kong

2003 2002 2001 2000 1999
12 11 10 9 8 7 6 5 4

Contents

Introduction

Course Organization

Move Up is a general English course which will take adult and young adult learners of English from starter level to advanced level. American English is used as the model for grammar, vocabulary, spelling, and pronunciation, but other varieties of English are included for listening and reading practice. The course components for each level are as follows:

For the student	For the teacher
Student's Book	Teacher's Book
Practice Book	Class Cassette
	Resource Pack

The Student's Book has twenty teaching lessons and four Progress Check lessons. After every five teaching lessons there is a Progress Check lesson to review the language covered in the preceding teaching lessons and to present new language work relevant to the grammar, functions, and topics covered so far. Within the teaching lessons the main grammar or language functions and the most useful vocabulary are presented in boxes that allow easy access to the principal language of the lesson. This makes the focus of the lesson clearly accessible for purposes of presentation and review. Each lesson will take between 60 and 90 minutes.

The Class Cassette contains the recorded material used in the Student's Book.

The Practice Book has twenty practice lessons corresponding to the twenty teaching lessons in the Student's Book. The Practice Book extends work done in class with the Student's Book, by providing further practice in grammar, vocabulary, reading, and writing. The activities are designed for self-access work and can be used either in the class or as self-study material. Each lesson will take between 45 and 60 minutes.

The Teacher's Book contains a presentation of the course design, methodological principles, as well as detailed teaching notes. It also includes two photocopiable tests. The teaching notes for each lesson include a step-by-step guide to teaching the lesson, a discussion of some of the difficulties the learners may encounter, and more detailed methodological issues arising from the material presented. The Practice Book Answer Key is in the Teacher's Book and may be photocopied.

The Resource Pack provides extra teaching material to practice the main language points of the teaching lessons. *Move Up* is designed to be very flexible in order to meet the very different requirements of learners. The Resource Pack contains a wide variety of communicative practice activities in the form of photocopiable worksheets with step-by-step Teacher's Notes on the back. There is at least one activity for each lesson in the Student's Book and the activities can be used to extend a core teaching lesson of 60–90 minutes from the Student's Book with an average of 30 minutes of extra material for use in the classroom. They can also be used to review specific structures, language, or vocabulary later in the course.

As well as step-by-step Teacher's Notes for each activity, the Resource Pack includes an introduction which explains how to use the worksheets and offers tips on how to get the most out of the activities.

Course Design

The course design is based on a broad and integrated multi-syllabus approach. It is broad in the sense that it covers grammar and language functions, vocabulary, reading, listening, speaking, writing, and sounds explicitly, and topics, learner training, and socio-cultural competence implicitly. It is integrated in that each strand of the course design forms the overall theme of each lesson. The lessons always include activities focusing on grammar and language functions, and vocabulary. They also include reading, listening, speaking, writing, and sounds. The inclusion of each strand of the syllabus is justified by its communicative purpose within the activity sequence. The methodological principles and approaches to each strand of course design are discussed opposite.

Methodological Principles

Here is an outline of the methodological principles for each strand of the course design.

Grammar and Language Functions

Many teachers and learners feel safe with grammar and language functions. Some learners may claim that they want or need grammar, although at the same time suggest that they don't enjoy it. Some teachers feel that their learners' knowledge of grammar is demonstrable proof of language acquisition. But this is only partly true. Mistakes of grammar are more easily tolerated than mistakes of vocabulary, as far as comprehension is concerned, and may be more acceptable than mistakes of socio-cultural competence, as far as behavior and effective communication is concerned. *Move Up* attempts to establish grammar and language functions in their pivotal position but without neglecting the other strands of the multi-syllabus design.

Vocabulary

There are two important criteria for the inclusion of words in the vocabulary boxes. Firstly, they are words which the elementary learner should acquire in order to communicate successfully in a number of social or transactional situations. Secondly, they may also be words which are generated by the reading or listening material, and are considered suitable for the elementary level. However, an overriding principle operates: there is usually an activity which allows learners to focus on and, one hopes, acquire the words which are personally relevant to them. This involves a process of personal selection or grouping of words according to personal categories. It is hard to acquire words which one doesn't need, so this approach responds to the learner's individual requirements and personal motivation. *Move Up* Elementary presents approximately 800 words in the vocabulary boxes for the learner's active attention, but each learner must decide which words to focus on. The *Wordbank* in the Practice Book encourages students to store the words they need in categories which are relevant to them.

Reading

The reading passages are at a slightly higher level than one might expect for learners at elementary level. Foreign language users who are not of near-native speaker competence are constantly confronted with difficult language, and to expose the learners to examples of real-life English in the reassuring context of the classroom is to help prepare them for the conditions of real life. There is always an activity or two which encourages the learner to respond to the passage either on a personal level or to focus on its main ideas. *Move Up* attempts to avoid a purely pedagogical approach and encourages the learner to respond to the passages in a personal and genuine way before using it for other purposes.

Listening

Listening is based on a similar approach to reading in *Move Up*. Learners are often exposed to examples of natural, authentic English in order to prepare them for real-life situations in which they will have to listen to ungraded English. But the tasks are always graded for the learners' particular level. A number of different native and non-native accents are used in the listening passages, to reflect the fact that in real life, very few speakers using English speak standard American pronunciation.

Speaking

Many opportunities are given for speaking, particularly in pairwork and groupwork. Learners are encouraged to work in pairs and groups because the number of learners in most classes does not allow the teacher to give undivided attention to each learner's English. In these circumstances, it is important for the teacher to evaluate whether fluency or accuracy is the most important criterion. On most occasions in *Move Up* Elementary, speaking practice in the *Grammar* sections is concerned with accuracy, and in the *Speaking* sections with fluency. In the latter case, it is better not to interrupt and correct the learners until after the activity is ended.

Writing

The writing activities in *Move Up* are based on guided paragraph writing with work on making notes, turning notes into sentences, and joining sentences into paragraphs with various linking devices. The activities are quite tightly controled. This is not to suggest that more creative work is not valid, but it is one of the responsibilities of a coursebook to provide a systematic grounding in the skill. More creative writing is covered in the Practice Book. Work is also done on punctuation, and most of the writing activities are based on real-life tasks, such as writing letters and cards.

Sounds

Pronunciation, stress, and intonation work tends to interrupt the communicative flow of a lesson, and there is a temptation to leave it out in the interests of maintaining the momentum of an activity sequence. In *Move Up* there is work on sounds in most lessons, usually just before the stage where the learners have to use the new structures orally in pairwork or groupwork. At this level, it seems suitable to introduce the basic system of English phonemes, most of which the learners will be able to reproduce accurately because similar phonemes exist in their own language, and activities which focus on stress in words and sentences, and on the implied meaning of certain intonation patterns, are included. The model for pronunciation is standard American English.

Topics

The main topics covered in *Move Up* Elementary include personal identification, house and home, daily life, leisure activities, travel, relations with other people, health, education, shopping, food and drink, geographical location, and the environment. On many occasions the words presented in the vocabulary box all belong to a particular word field or topic.

Learner Training

Implicit in the overall approach is the development of learner training to encourage learners to take responsibility for their own learning. Examples of this are regular opportunities to use monolingual and bilingual dictionaries, ways of organizing vocabulary according to personal categories, and inductive grammar work.

Cross-cultural Training

Much of the material and activities in *Move Up* creates the opportunity for cross-cultural training. Most learners will be using English as a medium of communication with other non-native speakers, and certainly with people of different cultures. Errors of socio-cultural competence are likely to be less easily tolerated than errors of grammar or lexical insufficiency. But it is impossible to give the learners enough specific information about a culture, because it is impossible to predict all the cultural circumstances in which they will use their newly acquired language competence. Information about *sample* cultures, such as the United States and Britain, as well as non-native English speaking ones, is given to allow the learners to compare their own culture with another. This creates opportunities for learners to reflect on their own culture in order to become more aware of the possibility of different attitudes, behavior, customs, traditions, and beliefs in other cultures. In this spirit, cross-cultural training is possible even with groups where the learners all come from the same cultural background. There are interesting and revealing differences between people from the same region or town, or even between friends and members of the same family. Exploring these will help the learners become not merely proficient at the language but competent in the overall aim of communication.

Level and Progress

One important principle behind *Move Up* is that the learners arrive at elementary level with very different language abilities and requirements. Some learners may find the early lessons very easy and will be able to move quickly on to later lessons. The way *Move Up* is structured, with individual lessons of 60-90 minutes, means that these learners can confirm that they have acquired a certain area of grammar, language function, and vocabulary, consolidate this competence with activities giving practice in the other aspects of the course design, and then move on. Others may find that their previous language competence needs to be reactivated more carefully and slowly. The core teaching lesson in the Student's Book may not provide them with enough practice material to ensure that the given grammar, language functions, and vocabulary have been firmly acquired. For these learners, extra practice may be needed and is provided in both the Practice Book (for self-study work) and the Resource Pack (for classroom work).

Interest and Motivation

Another important principle in the course design is the intrinsic interest of the materials. Interesting material motivates the learners, and motivated learners acquire the lanaguage more effectively. The topics have been carefully selected so that they are interesting to adults and young adults, with a focus on areas which would engage their general leisure-time interests. This is designed to generate what might be described as authentic motivation, the kind of motivation we have when we read a newspaper or watch a TV show. But it is obvious that we cannot motivate all learners all of the time. They may arrive at a potentially motivating lesson with little desire to learn on this particular occasion, perhaps for reasons that have nothing to do with the teacher, the course, or the material. It is therefore necessary to introduce tasks which attract what might be described as pedagogic or artificial motivation, tasks which would not usually be performed in real life, but which engage the learner in an artificial but no less effective way.

Variety of Material and Language

Despite the enormous amount of research done on language acquisition, no one has come up with a definitive description of how we acquire either our native language or a foreign language which takes account of every language learner or the teaching style of every teacher. Every learner has different interests and different requirements, and every teacher has a different style and approach to what they teach. *Move Up* attempts to adopt an approach which appeals to differing styles of learning and teaching. The pivotal role of grammar and vocabulary is reflected in the material but not at the expense of the development of the skills or pronunciation. An integrated multi-syllabus course design, designed to respond to the broad variety of learners' requirements and teachers' objectives, is at the heart of *Move Up*'s approach.

RESEARCH

Heinemann ELT is committed to continuing research into coursebook development. Many teachers contributed to the evolution of *Move Up* through piloting and reports, and we now want to continue this process of feedback by inviting users of *Move Up*— both teachers and students—to tell us about their experience of working with the course. If you or your colleagues have any comments, queries, or suggestions, please address them to the Publisher, Adult Group, Heinemann ELT, Halley Court, Jordan Hill, Oxford OX2 8EJ or contact your local Heinemann representative.

Map of the Book

Lesson	Grammar and functions	Vocabulary	Skills and sounds
1 *What's Your Name?* Introducing yourself	Present simple (1): *to be* Asking and saying who people are and where they're from	Countries	**Reading:** reading for main ideas **Listening:** listening for main ideas **Sounds:** syllable stress **Speaking:** asking and saying who you are and where you are from
2 *This Is Bruno and Maria* Jobs and countries	Present simple (2): *to be* Possessive adjectives Articles (1): *a/an*	Jobs	**Sounds:** syllable stress **Reading:** reading for main ideas **Writing:** writing a description saying who people are, where they are from, and what their job is
3 *Questions, Questions* Personal information	Questions Negatives Short answers	Forms giving personal information	**Listening:** listening for specific information **Speaking:** using a model dialogue for guided speaking practice **Writing:** completing a form; joining two pieces of information with *and*
4 *How Many Students Are There?* A brochure for a language school	*There is/are* Plurals (1): regular Position of adjectives	Numbers Classroom vocabulary Adjectives to describe people or things	**Sounds:** pronunciation of numbers **Reading:** reading for specific information **Speaking:** talking about your ideal school **Writing:** writing a brochure for your ideal school
5 *Where's My Pen?* Personal possessions	*Has/have* Prepositions of place (1)	Personal possessions Colors	**Listening:** listening for context; listening for specific information **Speaking:** talking about personal possessions
Progress Check Lessons 1–5	Review	Organizing new vocabulary Expressions to use when you don't understand	**Sounds:** syllable stress **Reading:** reading for main ideas **Writing:** punctuation of sentences
6 *Families* Family relationships	Possessive *'s* and *s'* Plurals (2): regular and irregular	Members of the family	**Reading:** predicting; reading for main ideas; inferring **Speaking:** talking about your family
7 *What Time Is It?* Customs around the world at different times of the day	Present simple (3) for customs and routines Prepositions of time (1)	Times of day Meals	**Speaking:** telling the time **Reading:** reading for main ideas **Listening:** listening for specific information **Writing:** writing an informal letter
8 *Home* The home of a family in Russia	*Some* and *any* (1) Prepositions of place (2)	Rooms Furniture Parts of the house	**Reading:** reading for specific information **Listening:** predicting; listening for specific information **Writing:** completing a chart about different homes
9 *How Do You Relax?* Different ways of relaxing	Present simple (4) for habits and routines *Wh-* questions Third person singular (*he/she/it*)	Hobbies	**Reading:** reading for specific information **Sounds:** third person singular present simple endings, /s/, /z/, /ɪz/ **Listening:** listening for specific information **Speaking:** talking about ways of relaxing in your free time
10 *Do You Like Jazz?* Different kinds of entertainment	Pronouns Present simple (5): talking about likes and dislikes	Entertainment and recreation	**Reading:** reading for main ideas; reading for specific information **Listening:** listening for main ideas; listening for specific information **Writing:** writing an advert for a penfriend
Progress Check Lessons 6–10	Review	Parts of speech Noting down new vocabulary	**Sounds:** /s/ and /z/; polite intonation **Reading:** reading for main ideas **Speaking:** talking about lifestyles in the United States and in your country
11 *A Day In My Life* A day in the life of a TV presenter	Present simple (6): saying how often you do things Prepositions of time (2)	Everyday actions	**Reading:** reading for main ideas; understanding text organisation **Speaking:** talking about your typical day **Listening:** listening for specific information **Writing:** writing about a typical day in your life using *then*, *after that*, and *and*

Lesson	Grammar and functions	Vocabulary	Skills and sounds
12 *How Do You Get to Work?* Different means of transport	Articles (2): *a/an, the,* and no article Talking about travel	Means of transport Adjectives and their opposites	**Reading:** reading for main ideas; reading for specific information **Speaking:** talking about how to get to work/school **Writing:** writing a paragraph on how to get to work/school
13 *Can You Swim?* Talking about what people can and can't do	*Can* and *can't* Questions and short answers	Skills and abilities	**Reading:** reading and answering a questionnaire **Listening:** listening for specific information; listening for context **Speaking:** talking about personal abilities
14 *How Do I Get to Lincoln Street?* Finding your way around a town	Prepositions of place (3) Asking for and giving directions	Shops and town facilities	**Listening:** listening for specific information; listening for main ideas **Reading:** predicting; reading for main ideas; reading for specific information **Speaking:** talking about shopping in the United States and your country
15 *What's Happening?* Describing actions taking place at the moment	Present continuous	Compass points Adjectives to describe places	**Listening:** listening for main ideas; listening for specific information **Speaking:** talking about cities around the world **Writing:** writing a postcard to a friend
Progress Check Lessons 11–15	Review	International words Words from other languages Words and expressions used in everyday situations	**Sounds:** /ð/ and /θ/; /ɑː/, /æ/, and /ʌ/; stressed words **Writing:** writing addresses **Speaking:** asking for and giving addresses
16 *Who Was Your First Friend?* Talking about childhood	Past simple (1): *be*	Adjectives to describe character	**Speaking:** talking about childhood **Listening:** listening for main ideas; listening for specific information **Sounds:** strong and weak forms of *was* **Writing:** writing true and false statements about your childhood
17 *How About Some Oranges?* Typical food at different meals	*Some* and *any* (2) Countable and uncountable nouns Making suggestions	Items of food and drink	**Listening:** listening for specific information; listening for main ideas **Sounds:** /s/ and /z/ in plural nouns **Speaking:** talking about eating conventions in the United States and your country
18 *Born in the U.S.A.* Biographies of Bruce Springsteen and Whitney Houston	Past simple (2): regular verbs *Have*	Words connected with the music business Important life events	**Reading:** predicting; reading for specific information **Sounds:** past simple endings: /t/, /d/, and /ɪd/ **Listening:** predicting; listening for specific information **Speaking:** talking about the life of a famous person
19 *What Does He Look Like?* Talking about appearance	Describing people	Adjectives to describe people's appearance Physical features	**Writing:** writing a letter giving a personal description **Listening:** listening for main ideas; listening for specific information **Speaking:** talking about typical appearance
20 *A Tour of Asia* Visiting cities in Asia	Past simple (3): irregular verbs *Yes/no* questions and short answers	Verbs connected with tourism Irregular verbs	**Sounds:** pronunciation of some Asian cities and countries **Listening:** listening for main ideas; listening for specific information **Speaking:** talking about a holiday
Progress Check Lessons 16–20	Review	Word association Words formed from other parts of speech	**Sounds:** /ɔː/, /ɜ/, and /ɒ/; silent letter patterns; interested intonation in sentences **Speaking:** playing a game called Twenty Questions

1

GENERAL COMMENTS

Move Up Elementary

This level of the *Move Up* series assumes that the learners have already had some formal instruction in English, or have been exposed to the language at some time in the past. The students will be encouraged to reactivate their passive knowledge of the language, but they will also be given the opportunity to study the basic elements of English grammar and vocabulary again. Point out to them that the target grammar and vocabulary of each lesson is clearly signposted in the two boxes: in this lesson, the main focus is on the present simple (1): *to be*, asking and saying who people are and where they come from, and on the towns and countries in the *Vocabulary and Sounds* section.

Names

This first lesson naturally focuses on names, and before it begins, you need to be clear what you would like to call your students and what you would like them to call you. Should it be family names or first names? The answer is whichever is the most socio-culturally appropriate.

READING AND LISTENING

1. Aim: to prepare for listening; to present the target structures.

● Point to yourself and say who you are and where you're from. If you have any pictures of famous people, hold them up in front of you and pretend to be these people. For the moment, it isn't necessary to ask the students to use the structures for themselves. Until they have more confidence, they can just listen and absorb the sounds of English.

● Ask the students to match the sentences and the people. They should look for physical clues to perform this activity.

Answers
a. picture 3
b. picture 2
c. picture 1
d. picture 4

2. Aim: to practice reading and listening.

● 🔲 This dialogue is the target conversation for this lesson. Ask students to read and listen as you play the tape. You may play the tape several times.

● Use the dialogue for pronunciation practice if you think the students are ready to speak. Act out the conversation with one or two students, then ask them to work in pairs and continue to act it out.

3. Aim: to practice reading for text organization.

● This kind of scrambled sentence activity allows the students to focus on the internal logic of a piece of spoken or written English, why one sentence goes in one position but rarely in another. Ask the students to read the sentences and number them in the order in which they go.

● Don't give the answer until they have listened to the conversation in activity 4.

● Ask pairs of students to act out the conversation for the whole class.

4. Aim: to practice listening; to check comprehension.

● 🔲 Ask the students to listen and check their answers to activity 3.

Answers
1. Hello. What's your name?
2. Hello, my name's Mei Ling. What's your name?
3. I'm Kazu. Where are you from, Mei Ling?
4. I'm from Taipei. And you?
5. I'm from Osaka.

GRAMMAR AND FUNCTIONS

1. Aim: to present the present simple of the verb *to be*; to focus on word order.

● Ask the students to read the information in the grammar box and then to do the activities.

● The students will already have seen the target structure in the *Reading and Listening* activities. This activity is designed to focus on its components and their position. Ask the students to write the sentences out with the words in the right order. You can also do this activity orally in pairs.

Answers
1. Hello, I'm Manuel.
2. Where are you from?
3. What's your name?
4. I'm from Los Angeles.
5. Hello, my name's Toni.
6. My name's Hannah.

● You may need to check your students' punctuation. You may also need to explain that *'s* and *'m* are the abbreviated forms of *is* and *am*, and both are not only perfectly acceptable but extremely common in spoken and informal written English.

2. **Aim: to practice using the target structure.**
- Explain that the sentences in activity 1 are two sides of a dialogue. Ask the students to match the sentences.

Answers
1 – 5, 2 – 4, 3 – 6

- You may like to explore other possible matches.

3. **Aim: to practice asking and saying who people are and where they're from.**
- Ask the students to do this activity orally in pairs.

Answers
1. What is your name?
2. Where are you from?
3. I'm from China.
4. My name is Peter.
5. Hello, I'm Joanna.
6. Where are you from?

VOCABULARY AND SOUNDS

1. **Aim: to present the English words for some common cities and countries.**
- Write the words *cities* and *countries* on the board and write a few words in the correct column. Ask students to suggest where the other words should go. Continue with other cities and countries which are not in the box. Try to focus on those places, such as neighboring cities, towns, and countries, that you're going to use often in class.

2. **Aim: to focus on syllable stress.**
- You may like to tell your students that English is a stress-timed language, in which the stress can change from syllable to syllable, and not a syllable-timed language, where there is equal stress on each syllable. Ask them if their language is stress- or syllable-timed.

- 🔊 Ask the students to say the words out loud as they listen to the tape. Ask the students to count the number of syllables in each word.

Answers
two syllables: Thailand, Bangkok, Japan
three syllables: Tokyo, Canada, Australia

3. **Aim: to focus on the spelling and pronunciation of the students' own towns and countries.**
- If the words for the students' towns and countries are very different in pronunciation and spelling, take some time in getting the students to say them out loud.

4. **Aim: to practice the pronunciation of the target structures.**
- 🔊 Play the tape and ask the students to listen and repeat the target structures.

SPEAKING

Aim: to practice using the target structures.
- Ask the students to ask and say who they are and where they're from. They should do this with as many people as possible. Encourage them to get up and walk around the classroom, if this is appropriate or possible.

- As an additional activity you may like to make a list of famous people on the board, and ask the students to suggest additions to it. Ask the students to say where the famous people are from, and write these places by the names.

- Ask the students to "become" one of these famous people, and to continue practicing the structures learned in this lesson, by going around and saying who they are and where they're from.

- If this is the first time the students have worked together, it might be a good idea for them to write a seating plan of the class with the names of every student. If they can't remember everyone's name, they can go and ask him or her again.

2

GENERAL COMMENTS

Course Design

Remind the students that *Move Up* has two principal syllabuses: grammar/functions and vocabulary, and a series of secondary syllabuses: reading, writing, speaking, listening, and sounds. Every lesson will contain the principal syllabuses. There are usually ten or twelve words in each vocabulary box. These are the words which are considered suitable to be learned at this level, and at this stage of the course. There may be other words which occur and which the students want to note down, but you should limit this, as too much vocabulary will simply be forgotten. The secondary syllabuses are often combined with one another, which reflects the fact that it is rare for them to be used in complete isolation.

Jobs

Many words for jobs are similar in different languages, so make a list of these before you come to the class.

VOCABULARY AND SOUNDS

1. Aim: to present some of the words in the vocabulary box.

● The words in the box are some of the most common jobs, but you may wish to supplement this list with jobs which are personally relevant to the students, such as their own or their parents' occupations.

● Ask the students to complete the sentences with words from the box.

> **Answers**
> He's an engineer.
> She's a doctor.
> He's a waiter.

● You may like to reinforce the process of acquiring these words by asking the students to categorize them under different headings, for example white/blue collar, high/low pay, male/female, etc.

2. Aim: to present the rest of the words in the vocabulary box.

● Ask the students to turn to the Communication Activity and check that they know what the other jobs are.

3. Aim: to focus on syllable stress in words.

● Ask the students to say the words out loud. For the moment, don't correct their pronunciation.

● 🔲 Play the tape. Ask the students to listen and check their pronunciation and the placing of the stress. This will force them to listen more attentively to the pronunciation.

4. Aim: to focus on the pronunciation of the words.

● 🔲 Play the tape again. Ask the students to listen and repeat the words.

● When you've played the tape several times, ask individual students to read out the list of words to the rest of the class.

READING

1. Aim: to prepare for reading.

● Explain that it is often useful to prepare for reading in a foreign language by making predictions about what you're about to read. It's something we do naturally and quickly in our own language but which may need to be done more consciously in a foreign language.

● Ask the students to predict where the three people might be from.

> **Answers**
> Brazil – 1
> Japan – 2
> United States – 3

2. Aim: to practice reading for main ideas.

● This micro skill is an important one to develop, particularly when the students deal with more complex passages. This activity is very simple, but will give practice in a kind of reading which will become more and more common as the learning process proceeds.

> **Answers**
> A – 3   B – 1   C – 2

3. Aim: to check comprehension.

● These questions are designed to encourage the students to take a closer look at the passages.

● You can do this activity orally with the whole class, or as pairwork.

> **Answers**
> 1. Pete's from Iowa.
> 2. He's an engineer.
> 3. Bruno and Maria are from São Paulo.
> 4. They are doctors.
> 5. Michiko is from Tokyo.
> 6. She's a teacher.

● Point out that in reply to the question *Where are you from?* the answer can be either a town or a country. Both take the preposition *from*.

GRAMMAR

1. Aim: to focus on the forms of the verb *to be*.

● Ask the students to read the information in the grammar box and then to do the exercises.

● This activity encourages the students to think about the form of the verb *to be*. It acknowledges the fact that students sometimes mix up *am, is,* and *are*, but focuses on the limits of the potential confusion.

Answers
Three: *am, is, are*

2. Aim: to focus on questions and answers.

● You can check this activity orally with the whole class.

Answers
1. d 2. a 3. e 4. c 5. b

3. Aim: to focus on the use of articles with jobs; to focus on the use of *a* and *an*.

● Tell the students that the indefinite article is always required before a job. Ask students to think of a job and go around asking and saying what their jobs are.
I'm a businessman.
NOT *I'm businessman.*

● Make sure the students use *an* before words which begin with a vowel.

Answers
1. an 2. a 3. an 4. a 5. a 6. a

WRITING

Aim: to practice writing; to practice using the target structures.

● This is the first writing activity of *Move Up* Elementary and you may want to tell the students about your grading policy. Decide if you're going to encourage accuracy or fluency in writing, or both at different times. Show them the symbols you use to indicate wrong words, words in the wrong position, missing words, spelling mistakes, grammar mistakes, etc.

● Ask the students to write descriptions of the two people.

Answers
1. This is Sheila Smith. She's from Melbourne in Australia. She's a student.
2. This is Rosario Barbisan. He's from Montevideo in Uruguay. He's a teacher.

● As an additional activity you could ask the students to write similar paragraphs about people they know. They should say who they are, where they're from, and what their job is.

● You may like to ask the students to do this activity for homework.

3
GENERAL COMMENTS

Questions

In some languages, it is possible to ask a question by making a statement with a particular intonation. This is possible in English, but it is more common to use a question form with suitable intonation. The word order in questions often causes students difficulty, as does the correct use of the auxiliary. This lesson focuses on questions with the verb *to be*, which can be formed by a question word and/or a simple inversion. Care in establishing the rules and plenty of practice is advisable at this stage if you want your students to avoid common mistakes later on.

Fluency and Accuracy

You may like to point out the distinction between fluency and accuracy and how a shift from one to the other will occur at different stages in the lesson and in the course. You may want to point out that, at this early stage, when the students have relatively little language, the language practice will focus mainly on accuracy, but that at a later stage you will not want to correct them every time they make a mistake, in order to develop their fluency in English.

LISTENING AND SPEAKING

1. **Aim: to prepare for listening.**
- Explain to the students that they are going to read the first part of a conversation.

- Ask the students to read and listen to the first part and decide who is speaking and if they know each other.

- You may like to ask the students to act out the first part of the conversation.

- Point out that a common response to *How are you?* is *Fine, thanks, how are you?* You usually greet someone with these expressions when you know them or have met them before. For people you meet for the first time, you say *How do you do?* and you reply *How do you do?* Neither form is really a question, more a formulaic exchange.

2. **Aim: to prepare for listening; to practice reading for text organization.**
- It would be possible simply to give the students the transcript of the conversation they are about to hear, and to follow it as they listen. However, this activity helps the students to focus on the organization of the conversation, and to prepare for listening by doing some careful reading.

- 📼 Ask the students to decide where the sentences go. When they have finished, play the tape and ask them to check their answers.

> **Answers**
> 1. a 2. c 3. d 4. b 5. e

3. **Aim: to practice speaking.**
- Ask the students to act out the conversation in pairs.

- Ask two or three pairs to perform the conversation in front of the whole class.

GRAMMAR

1. Aim: to focus on negatives.

- Ask the students to read the information in the grammar box and then to do the activities.

- Ask the students to look back at the conversation in *Listening and Speaking* activities 1 and 2, and to mark the statements in this activity true (T) or false (F).

Answers
1. T   2. F   3. T   4. F   5. T   6. T

2. Aim: to practice using questions and short answers.

- Ask the students to match the questions with the answers.

Answers
1. b   2. a   3. d   4. c   5. e

3. Aim: to practice writing short answers.

- Make sure the students realize that the questions are directed at them, and they should answer honestly.

VOCABULARY AND WRITING

1. Aim: to present the words in the vocabulary box.

- The words in the vocabulary box are those which are commonly found on forms, such as Landing Cards, which you often need to complete when you enter a foreign country.

- You may want to write your name and other details on the board, to make the meaning clear. Of course, you don't have to tell them your first name or any other inappropriate information. This may be a suitable moment to teach *Mr., Mrs., Miss,* and *Ms.* (pronounced /mz/).

Answers
1. last name   2. first name   3. job   4. age
5. address   6. phone number   7. married

- You may like to explain that in most English-speaking contexts, if someone asks you your name, you give your first name followed by your last name. Another expression for *last name* in English is *family name* or *surname*.

- Tell the students that in the United States it is very common for people to use first names, even between, for example, a boss and an employee, or an older and a younger person. If they are invited to use first names, they should do so even if they feel uncomfortable with such apparent informality.

2. Aim: to provide a model for writing.

- Ask the students to complete this description with the information on the Landing Card.

Answers
Greg Sheppard is an actor and he's 23. His address is 365 Avenue of the Americas, New York, and his phone number is (212) 693-4428. He isn't married.

- You may like to point out that the parentheses around the 212 in the phone number show that you do not need to dial these numbers if you're calling within New York.

4

GENERAL COMMENTS

Numbers

The presentation and practice of numbers in this lesson assumes that this is not the first time students have encountered them in English. You may want to give a lot more extra practice than there is space for in the Student's Book. Take a look at the practice activities in the Practice Book and the Resource Pack for ideas.

Reading

The text in this lesson has been carefully written so that all the language is comprehensible to the student at this stage of the course. However, other texts in *Move Up* Elementary are at a level slightly higher than your students might expect. This is deliberate and is designed to help them develop their reading skills and their ability to deal with difficult words, such as they will have to do in real-life contexts, in the supportive environment of the classroom.

SOUNDS AND VOCABULARY

1. Aim: to present the pronunciation of numbers 1–20.

● Write the numbers 1-20 on the board.

● ▭ Play the tape and ask the students to listen and repeat the numbers.

● Point to numbers on the board and ask individual students to say what the number is.

2. Aim: to present the written form of numbers.

● Ask the students to write the numbers.

● You may like to ask the students to check their answers in pairs before they turn to the Communication Activity.

3. Aim: to focus on the distinction between *-ty* and *-teen.*

● Say the words clearly several times.

● Ask the students to say the words out loud.

● Ask the students to match the stress patterns with the numbers.

> **Answers**
> ■ five six eight nine
> ■■ fifteen sixteen eighteen nineteen
> ■■■ seven fifty sixty eighty ninety
> Note: seventeen and seventy have three syllables so have different stress patterns.

● ▭ Play the tape and ask the students to check their answers. As they listen they can say the words out loud.

4. Aim: to present the vocabulary in the box.

● Students may already know some of these vocabulary items. You may like to point at certain items in your classroom, such as *cassette player, book, table, chair,* etc.

> **Answers**
> classroom, study room, cassette player, book, table, chair

5. Aim: to present the vocabulary in the box.

● This is the first time in *Move Up* Elementary that adjectives have been presented. Illustrate the function of an adjective (a word which gives extra information about a noun) by referring to adjectives in the students' own language.

● Ask the students to decide who or what the adjectives can be used to describe. This activity introduces the concept of collocations.

> **Possible Answers**
> **person:** friendly, beautiful, good, kind, interesting, popular
> **school:** friendly, international, good, popular
> **classroom:** interesting
> **town:** friendly, beautiful, international, interesting, popular
> **lesson:** good, interesting

READING

1. Aim: to practice reading for specific information.

● Explain that a brochure is a document used for purposes of publicizing a place or a service.

● Ask the students to read the text and answer the questions. Explain that they may not understand every word, and tell them that you'll explain only four words, so they must choose those words carefully.

2. Aim: to check comprehension.

● Ask the students to work in pairs and to check their answers.

> **Answers**
> 1. San Francisco
> 2. There are two hundred students from thirty countries.
> 3. Thirty
> 4. Mexico, Brazil, Japan, Thailand
> 5. Andy
> 6. (415) 343-8211

GRAMMAR

1. Aim: to elicit the rule for using *there is* and *there are*.

● Ask the students to read the information in the grammar box and then to do the activities.

● Do this activity orally with the whole class. It's often useful to get the students to work out the rule for themselves rather than simply give it to them.

Answers
1. *there is*
2. *there are*

2. Aim: to focus on regular plurals.

● Draw the students' attention to the fact that most plurals in English are formed by adding *-s* or *-es* to a noun.

● Ask the students to do the exercise.

Answers
1. computer, rooms
2. tables, chairs, cassette player
3. teachers
4. buildings
5. student

● Tell the students that you use *one* not *a/an* if the actual number is significant.

SPEAKING AND WRITING

1. Aim: to practice speaking and writing.

● This is an activity which involves a lot of speaking and a certain amount of writing. Encourage the students to plan their brochures very carefully, and to write them as a collaborative effort.

● You may like to ask the students to do this activity for homework.

2. Aim: to practice speaking; to encourage a response to other people's work.

● If you can, put the various brochures on the wall for everyone to read.

5

GENERAL COMMENTS

Has/have

Some students may have learned the alternative form *have got* to talk about possession. This is less commonly used in American English than in other varieties, and is therefore not introduced in this level of *Move Up*. The auxiliary verb *do* is introduced here to form questions and negatives but will be studied in greater detail in Lessons 7 and 9.

LISTENING AND VOCABULARY

1. Aim: to prepare for listening; to focus on the target structures.

● Ask the students to read the conversations and to complete them with the words. This pre-listening stage is designed to give them confidence when they listen to the tape.

2. Aim: to check comprehension; to listen for specific information.

● 🖭 Play the tape and ask the students to check their answers to 1.

> **Answers**
> 1. A Where's my pen?
>   B It's on the table, near your book.
>   A Oh, I see. Thanks.
>
> 2. A Do you have a cellular phone?
>   B Yes, I do. It's in my bag. Here you are.
>   A Thanks.
>
> 3. A Where's my bag?
>   B What color is it?
>   A It's blue.
>   B It's under your chair.
>   A Oh yes. Thank you.

3. Aim: to practice using the target structures.

● Act out the conversations with three students in front of the class.

● Ask several students to act out the conversations in pairs in front of the class.

● Ask the students to act out the conversations in pairs. They can change pairs each time.

4. Aim: to present the words in the vocabulary box.

● Ask the students to match the words in the box with the items in the picture.

● Check the students' answers with the whole class.

5. Aim: to present the words in the vocabulary box.

● It is easier to present the words for colors if you have some colored paper or some magazine pictures showing the relevant colors.

6. Aim: to practice using the words presented in this lesson.

● Ask the students to say what color the different items are in the picture.

● Continue this activity by pointing to objects in the classroom and saying what color they are.

● Ask the students to continue this activity in pairs.

> **Answers**
> pink bag, pink watch, brown comb,
> orange notebook, green pencil, black diary,
> yellow walkman, blue camera, black wallet,
> red book, purple glasses, black calculator,
> black cellular phone, brown jacket

GRAMMAR

1. **Aim: to focus on *has/have*.**

- Ask the students to read the information in the grammar box and then to do the activities.

- Tell the students two or three things you have in your bag or your pocket.

- Ask the students to do the same.

- Ask the students to work in pairs and say what they have in their bags. Once they've done this, they may like to work with different partners.

2. **Aim: to focus on prepositions of place.**

- Point out that the statements in the grammar box accurately describe the position of the objects in the drawing. Ask the students to decide if the statements in this activity are true or false.

Answers
All the statements are false.

- You may like to ask students to correct the statements.

3. **Aim: to practice using the target structures.**

- Ask the students to continue to practice using *has/have* and prepositions of place.

SPEAKING

1. **Aim: to practice speaking; to reactivate passive vocabulary.**

- Ask the students to suggest things that typical teenagers have in their country. Make a list on the board.

- Ask the students to work in pairs and add four or five items to the list. Ask them to add a comment such as *everyone, most people, a lot of people* by each item.

2. **Aim: to consolidate vocabulary learning.**

- This is a memory game. Ask the students to look at the picture in the Communication Activity. Allow them 30 seconds for this.

3. **Aim: to practice speaking; to practice using the target structures.**

- Ask the students to turn back to page 11, or to close their books.

- Ask the students to describe in detail what they saw and where the objects are. You can do this with the whole class.

- For homework, you may like to ask the students to write a list of what they saw and where it was.

Progress Check 1–5

GENERAL COMMENTS

You can work through this Progress Check in the order shown, or concentrate on areas which have caused difficulty in Lessons 1 to 5. You can also let the students choose the activities they would like or feel the need to do.

VOCABULARY

1. Aim: to organize vocabulary learning.
● Before you come to class, you may like to think about the notes you make or made when you came across new vocabulary. Share this experience and advice with your students.

● It may be a suitable moment to draw your students' attention to the *Wordbank* in their Practice Books.

● Encourage the learners to write the words down under the topic headings.

> **Possible Answers**
> **countries:** Australia, Brazil
> **jobs:** doctor, taxi driver
> **classroom:** book, pen
> **colors:** blue, red
> **personal possessions:** computer, diary, walkman
> **personal information:** age, female, first name

● Make sure the students understand that some words can go under more than one heading.

2. Aim: to develop communication strategies.
● Write the expressions on the board, and spend time getting the students to learn them by heart. Tell them not to worry about each component. In time, they'll understand how the expression is put together syntactically.

● Ask the students to choose words which they don't know, and to go around asking and saying what the words mean.

● If you haven't done so already, this is a good moment to point out that the target vocabulary in each lesson is contained in the vocabulary box, and that the students should make an effort to ensure they now know these words from Lessons 1 to 5.

GRAMMAR

1. Aim: to review asking for and giving personal information; to practice word order in sentences.

> **Answers**
> 1. My name's Pete.
> 2. Are you married?
> 3. How are you?
> 4. How many students are there?
> 5. What's your name?
> 6. The pen is on the table.

2. Aim: to review possessive adjectives and subject pronouns.

> **Answers**
> I – my, you – your, he – his, she – her,
> it – its, we – our, they – their

3. Aim: to review possessive adjectives and subject pronouns.

> **Answers**
> 1. She's
> 2. We're
> 3. My
> 4. His
> 5. You're
> 6. Their

4. Aim: to review questions.

> **Answers**
> 1. What's your name?
> 2. Where are you from?
> 3. What's your job?
> 4. What's her name?
> 5. Where's she from?
> 6. What's her job?

5. Aim: to review giving personal information.

> **Answers**
> 1. Paul Harris
> 2. 21 years old in 1997
> 3. Student
> 4. Seattle

6. Aim: to review *there is/are.*

● Ask the students to answer the questions with reference to their own classroom.

7. Aim: to review prepositions of place.

Answers
The coat is on the chair.
The bag is on the table.
The book is on the table.
The glasses are in the bag.

SOUNDS

1. Aim: to review stress patterns.

● ▱ Play the tape. Then ask the students to say the words out loud.

2. Aim: to review stress patterns.

● Ask the students to match the words with the stress patterns in activity 2.

● ▱ Play the tape so the students can check their answers.

Answers
■▪ mother teacher noisy people
▪■ police cassette
■▪▪ stereo camera

READING AND WRITING

1. Aim: to practice reading for specific information.

Answers
1. c   2. a   3. b

2. Aim: to practice using correct punctuation.

Answers
How many people speak English as a
foreign language?
100 million people speak it as a foreign language in
countries like Brazil, Japan, Korea, and Thailand.
Is there any other language with more speakers?
There are about 1 billion speakers of Chinese as a
first language.
How many words do people use in everyday
speech?
Most people only use about 10,000 words.

6

GENERAL COMMENTS

Apostrophe 's

It is possible that your students may become confused with the different uses of the ending -s and apostrophe 's . You may need to take time during this lesson to point out that:
- the plural of many nouns is formed by adding s.
- the apostrophe 's when added to he, she, or it is the contracted form of is.
- the apostrophe 's when added to a noun referring to a person and followed by another noun indicates the possessive 's .
- its is the possessive adjective and it's is the contracted form of it is.

The apostrophe is also used to show that a letter is missing in I'm = I am, aren't = are not, isn't = is not.

It may be interesting to reflect that the different uses of the apostrophe 's ending also cause confusion among native speakers of English. There are many examples of the so-called intrusive apostrophe used in straightforward plurals in everyday English, e.g.
Please have your bag's ready for inspection.
There is some speculation about whether we are witnessing a change in usage which will become standard in the years to come.

VOCABULARY

1. Aim: to review the words in the vocabulary box.
- It is very likely that your students will have come across the words for members of the family at some earlier stage, so this activity is designed as review. Ask the students to say the words out loud, and to check if they know what they mean.

- Tell the students that all the people are related, and ask them to guess who the people in the picture are using the words in the vocabulary box.

2. Aim: to check comprehension.
- In case the meaning of these words has escaped the students, this activity sends them to the back of the book to check that they know the exact meaning.

- Ask the students to work in pairs. They should turn to the Communication Activities as instructed and find out who the people in the picture are.

3. Aim: to check comprehension.
- Ask the students to say who the people are in relation to Holly.

Answers
Andrew is her brother.
Toni is her brother's wife.
David is her grandfather.
Philip is her father.
Steve is her brother.
Kate is her grandmother.
Jenny is her mother.

GRAMMAR

1. Aim: to focus on the distinction between possessive 's and contraction 's.
- Ask the students to read the information in the grammar box and then to do the activities.

- It may be a suitable moment to give your students the information provided in General Comments at the beginning of this lesson.

- To help your students, ask them to identify the part of speech of the words around the 's.

Answers
1. possessive
2. contraction
3. possessive
4. possessive
5. possessive
6. contraction, possessive

2. Aim: to practice putting the apostrophe in the correct position.

● Ask the students to read the passage and put the apostrophe in the right place.

> **Answers**
>
> My parents' names are Miguel and Paula. My mother's a journalist and my father's unemployed. I've got two brothers and a sister. My brothers' names are Pedro and Carlos. My sister's name's Patricia. She's married to Juan. She's a teacher and he's a banker.

3. Aim: to practice using the possessive 's.

● Ask the students to explain the meaning of these words using the possessive 's.

> **Possible Answers**
>
> **aunt:** my mother's sister or my father's sister
> **uncle:** my mother's brother or my father's brother
> **cousin:** my uncle and aunt's son or daughter
> **grandfather:** my mother's father or my
>   father's father
> **grandmother:** my mother's mother or my
>   father's mother

4. Aim: to practice talking about your family.

● Ask the students to write the names of their family and to ask and say who they are. Write the following on the board.

> *Jim is my brother*
> *Jim is my brother's name.*
> *My brother's name is Jim.*

● Encourage them to use different expressions as they describe their family.

READING AND SPEAKING

1. Aim: to prepare for reading.

● Ask the students to look at the picture of Kibiri and to decide where he comes from. You may like to spend some time teaching the names of a few countries in Africa. Write the countries on the board.

2. Aim: to prepare for reading.

● The underlined words are those which the students are likely to find difficult. You can ask them to look these up in their dictionaries or you can explain or translate them.

3. Aim: to practice reading for main ideas.

● Ask the students to read the passage and to decide which is Kibiri.

● Kibiri is standing in the middle of the picture. Do not be surprised if your students think that either of the men standing in this picture could be Kibiri. This is a speculative exercise aimed at generating the students' interest in the authentic passage.

> **Answer**
>
> Kibiri is standing in the middle of the picture, dressed in white.

4. Aim: to practice reading for specific information; to practice using the target structures.

● This activity is an opportunity for the students to read the passage again and to use the possessive 's to describe who the people in the picture are.

5. Aim: to practice speaking; to provide an opportunity for cross-cultural comparison.

● The intention of the passage about Kibiri was to offer a family profile which is very probably very different from that of the students' own families. Use this opportunity to explore the differences between Kibiri's family life and your students' own family life. What advantages and disadvantages are there?

● You may like to do this activity in your students' own language, as they may not yet be at a suitable level to do this in English. It may be worth pointing out at this stage that cross-cultural work of this kind can often be done in the students' own language.

7

GENERAL COMMENTS

You may like to tell your students that it isn't common to use the twenty-four hour clock in everyday spoken and written American English. The A.M./P.M. distinction is used if there is any ambiguity.

There may not be enough practice of telling the time in this lesson, and you may like to supplement it with activities from the Practice Book and the Resource Pack.

If you have a cardboard clock for teaching the time, you'll need it for this lesson.

SPEAKING AND VOCABULARY

1. Aim: to present the times of the day.

● 📼 Ask the students to look at the clocks and to listen to the tape. You can ask them to repeat the times as they hear them.

● Ask the students to write the times for the other clocks.

> **Answers**
> a. ten after twelve
> b. six thirty
> c. twenty-five to seven
> d. five to one
> e. twelve o'clock
> f. a quarter after two

● Ask the students to check their answers in pairs.

2. Aim: to practice telling the time.

● Write a few times of the day on the board. Say *Excuse me, what's the time?* Point to a student and elicit a reply.

● Ask the students to work in pairs and do the same.

3. Aim: to present the words in the vocabulary box.

● Ask the students to use their dictionaries if there are any words which they don't understand. You may also like to explain some of the words yourself, although find out if anyone else can do so first.

● Ask the students to complete the sentences with words from the box.

> **Answers**
> 1. breakfast
> 2. evening
> 3. go to bed
> 4. finish
> 5. weekend
> 6. lunch
> 7. morning
> 8. work, morning

READING AND LISTENING

1. Aim: to practice reading for main ideas.
- Ask the students to read the passage about daily routines around the world. Ask them to compare the daily routines with their own.

2. Aim: to practice speaking.
- Ask the students to work in pairs and to compare their answers. It doesn't matter if all your students come from the same culture. The activity is designed to create an opportunity for cross-cultural comparison.

3. Aim: to practice listening for main ideas.
- Ask the students to listen to Tony talking about the statements. They should simply check the statements which Tony says are true for Australia.

Answers

In Austria children go to school at seven thirty in the morning.	✗
In Japan people go to work between seven and nine in the morning.	✓
In Holland people start work at eight in the morning and finish work at five in the afternoon.	✗
In Greece children start school at eight and finish at one thirty or start at two and finish at seven in the evening.	✗
In Korea people have lunch at noon.	✗
In Mexico people have lunch at three or four o'clock in the afternoon.	✗
In the United States people finish work at five in the afternoon.	✓
In Norway people have dinner at five in the afternoon.	✗
In Chile people have dinner at ten or eleven in the evening.	✗

- Ask the students to check their answers in pairs.

GRAMMAR

1. Aim: to practice using the present simple affirmative and negative.
- Ask the students to read the information in the grammar box and then to do the activities.
- Ask the students to write sentences which are true for their country.

2. Aim: to focus on prepositions of time.
- The prepositions of time presented in this lesson are complicated by the fact that some of them are followed by the article, and some of them are not.

Answers
1. the 2. no article 3. the 4. no article 5. the

WRITING

1. Aim: to focus on conventions of writing informal letters; to prepare for letter writing.
- Make sure the students understand the differences between informal letters (to friends and family) and formal letters (in business situations, to your bank, etc.). Make it clear that this letter is an informal one, between two penfriends.
- Ask the students to answer the questions about the layout and other conventions. Make sure they realize that the address is that of the person sending the letter.

Answers
You start an informal letter with *Dear*, followed by the person's first name.
You write your address at the top of the letter on the right-hand side.
You write the date under your address.
You finish it with *Best wishes* and your name.

2. Aim: to practice informal letter writing; to practice using the target structures.
- The letter in 1 is intended to be used as a model for this activity.
- Ask the students to work in pairs and read the letter again. Ask them to brainstorm ideas to put into a similar letter describing daily routines in their own country.
- Ask the students to work on their own and to do a draft of their letters.
- When they are ready, they can look at each other's letters to make suggestions and to borrow ideas.
- Ask the students to do another draft or two of their letters. You may like to set this stage for homework.
- Put the letters on the wall for everyone to read.

8

GENERAL COMMENTS

Cross-cultural Comparison

As the Introduction mentioned, creating the opportunity for cross-cultural comparison is an important part of the syllabus for socio-cultural training. The cultures shown in the *Move Up* series are chosen for their interest value as well as for the opportunity they provide to allow the students to reflect on their own cultural background. Furthermore, even with students from the same background, there will be small differences in behavior, attitudes, customs, and beliefs which can be exploited in the classroom for their socio-cultural significance.

VOCABULARY

1. Aim: to present the words in the vocabulary box.
- Like the words to describe members of the family, these may also be words which the students already know, so you may not need to explain many of them. Ask other students to explain difficult words before you explain them yourself.

- Ask the students to work in pairs and to say what rooms there are in their homes.

- Remind the students that they learned the structure *there is/are* in Lesson 4.

- Ask three or four students to tell the whole class which rooms they have in their homes.

2. Aim: to present the words in the vocabulary box.
- Check everyone understands the meaning of the words.

- Ask the students to say in which rooms they would expect to see the words in the box.

> **Possible Answers**
> **living room:** armchair, bookshelf, chair, curtains, fireplace, lamp, rug, sofa, table, TV
> **dining room:** chair, curtains, rug, table
> **kitchen:** cabinet, dishwasher, refrigerator, table, sink, stove
> **bathroom:** bath, shower, toilet, sink
> **bedroom:** bed, cabinet, curtains
> **family room:** bookshelf, chair, lamp, rug, table

3. Aim: to present the words in the vocabulary box.
- Draw a ground plan of a house, and show where the street is. Label the ground plan *at the back, at the front, indoors, outdoors, in the yard*. Draw the front view of the house and label it *upstairs* and *downstairs*.

- Ask the students to say where the rooms in 1 are in their homes.

READING

Aim: to practice reading for specific information.

● Ask the students to read the information about the Kapralov family and look at the picture to decide if the statements are true or false.

Answers
1. False
2. False
3. True
4. False
5. True
6. False

GRAMMAR

1. **Aim: to focus on the use of *some* and *any*.**

● Ask the students to read the information in the grammar box and then to do the exercises.

● Do this activity orally with the whole class.

Answers
1. any   2. some   3. some
4. any   5. any   6. some

2. **Aim: to focus on the difference between *they're* and *their*.**

● Remind the students that:
their is a possessive adjective
they're is the contracted form of *they are*.
They are both pronounced in the same way as *there*.

Answers
1. They're   2. Their   3. They're
4. There   5. Their   6. There

3. **Aim: to present prepositions of place.**

● Ask students to look at the picture and see if they can say where things are. Remind them to use the prepositions *in front of* and *behind* in the instances where they can't see the various items.

Possible Answers
1. There's a bookshelf behind the TV.
2. There's a chair next to the TV.
3. There's a bookshelf behind the table.
4. There's a chair next to the table.
5. There's a rug in front of the sofa.
6. There's a mirror next to the house.

LISTENING AND WRITING

1. **Aim: to practice listening for specific information.**

● Ask the students to guess Jeff's answers to the statements in the chart.

● 🔲 Play the tape and ask the students to listen and check.

2. **Aim: to check comprehension.**

● Ask the students to work in pairs and to complete the chart.

Answers
Type of home: boat
Size: 35 feet long, 10 feet wide
Number of rooms: 5
Number of people: 3
Furniture: refrigerator, stove, several armchairs, a TV, a shower
Most important item: computer

● 🔲 Play the tape and ask the students to check their answers.

3. **Aim: to practice speaking.**

● Ask the students to talk about their own homes and to complete the chart.

● You may like to ask them to write a paragraph about their partner's home for homework.

9

GENERAL COMMENTS

Listening

Like the reading passages in *Move Up* Elementary, the listening passages contain a mixture of very carefully controled and graded language and roughly graded material, which may be slightly above the level which the student might expect. Listening comprehension is generally the skill which the students find most hard to acquire. Unlike reading, they are not in control of the rate of delivery when listening in a foreign language, and practice in this skill often generates a certain amount of panic and confusion. The students need to be reminded that in real life, they won't be able to understand every word of spoken English, and that it is a good idea to expose them to these circumstances in the reassuring and supportive context of the classroom.

VOCABULARY AND READING

1. Aim: to present the words and expressions in the vocabulary box.
- Ask the students to match the words in the box with the drawings.

> **Answers**
> a. eat an apple
> b. watch a baseball game
> c. take a shower
> d. go running
> e. listen to the radio
> f. drink coffee
> g. play guitar
> h. read a newspaper
> i. play soccer

2. Aim: to practice reading for main ideas.
- Ask three or four students to say how they relax. Encourage them to use words and expressions from the vocabulary box in 1.

- Ask the students to read the passage and to say who the people in the pictures are.

> **Answers**
> Carrie, Christchurch
> Tanya's husband, São Paulo

3. Aim: to check comprehension; to present the target structures.
- Ask the students to read the passage again and to find the answers to the questions.

- You may like to check the students' answers to the questions with the whole class.

> **Answers**
> 1. In San Fransisco.
> 2. He's a taxi driver.
> 3. In the evening.
> 4. Because his girlfriend likes television.
> 5. She takes a hot bath and listens to the radio.
> 6. Her husband.

GRAMMAR

1. Aim: to focus on the form of the third person singular.
- Ask the students to read the information in the grammar box and then to do the activities.

- Tell the students that the passage is mostly in the first person singular, but that there are some examples of the third person. Remind them to look for verbs ending in -*s* or -*es*.

> **Answers**
> goes, likes, reads, learns

2. Aim: to practice the third person singular ending.
- Ask the students to transform the first person singular verb endings into third person singular.

> **Answers**
> Seong Hyun goes running.
> Tanya sometimes goes with her husband to his club.
> Patricia takes a hot bath and listens to the radio.
> Karl Heinz plays the guitar.
> Daisuke watches a video with his girlfriend.
> Carrie drinks tea and eats toast and jam in the yard.
> Fiona eats chocolates while her boyfriend reads to her.
> Jerry learns languages.
> Newton never relaxes.

3. Aim: to focus on word order in question forms and the use of the auxiliary.
- The use of *do/does* in questions may cause students some difficulties, especially for those whose language uses a simple inversion to form a question. Explain that the use of the auxiliary verb in English is not optional. It has to be used when you ask a *wh-* question.
- Ask the students to complete the sentences.

> **Answers**
> 1. does, do   2. go   3. What, like
> 4. does, watch   5. Where, eat   6. does, relax

4. Aim: to practice using the third person singular.
- Ask the students to work in pairs and ask and answer the questions in 3.

> **Answers**
> 1. She goes running.
> 2. He goes to his club.
> 3. He likes the *Rolling Stones*.
> 4. He watches a video with his girlfriend.
> 5. She drinks tea and eats toast in the yard.
> 6. Because he's a taxi driver.

5. Aim: to practice speaking; to practice using the present simple for habits and routines.
- Ask the students to talk in pairs about what they like doing to relax.

SOUNDS

1. Aim: to focus on the pronunciation of third person singular endings.
- Ask the students to listen as you say the three verbs out loud. Emphasize the endings.
- 🔲 Play the tape and ask the students to repeat the verbs.

2. Aim: to focus on the pronunciation of third person singular endings.
- Write the three phonemes on the board. Ask the students to say the verbs out loud, and then ask students to come up and write the verb under the correct phoneme.
- 🔲 Play the tape. The students check their answers.

> **Answers**
> /s/: makes, eats, drinks, likes
> /z/: lives, listens, plays, reads
> /ɪz/: finishes, washes

LISTENING AND SPEAKING

1. Aim: to prepare for listening.
- This activity can also be used to pre-teach any difficult items.
- Ask the students to check the things they do in their free time.

2. Aim: to practice listening for main ideas.
- 🔲 Play the tape and ask the students to check the things Helen and Chris do.

	Helen	Chris
go to the movies		
watch TV		✓
listen to the radio		
play sports		
learn a language	✓	
play music		
read a book	✓	
visit friends		✓
go to a club		✓

3. Aim: to practice the target structures.
- Ask the students to check their answers on the chart. Make sure they are formulating third person singular sentences correctly.

4. Aim: to check comprehension.
- 🔲 Play the tape again and ask the students to check their answers.
- You may like to ask the students to write a few sentences for homework, describing what Helen and Chris do to relax.

10

GENERAL COMMENTS

Like + *-ing* or Noun

This lesson briefly presents the language for talking about likes and dislikes. You may like to explain that the *-ing* form of verbs operates just like a noun phrase. These structures will be further explored in *Move Up* Pre-intermediate.

Topicality

It is impossible for a textbook such as *Move Up* to remain topical for the whole of its life. It's important, therefore, to see this lesson as a blueprint for discussion, and to replace any outmoded references with more topical ones.

VOCABULARY AND READING

1. Aim: to present the words in the vocabulary box.
- This lesson overlaps in subject matter with Lesson 9. Some of the expressions learned in that lesson can also be used in this one, so take every opportunity for review.

- Check that everyone understands the words in the vocabulary box. Ask other students to explain any difficult words, if necessary.

2. Aim: to focus on the difference between nouns and *-ing* form words.
- Ask the students to put the words in two columns.

> **Answers**
> **nouns:** football, baseball, magazines, classical music, jazz, rock music, Chinese food
> ***-ing* words and phrases:** cooking, going to parties, swimming, dancing, going to the theater, going to the movies, watching sports

- Ask the students to think of other expressions using the same words. For example, *watching soccer, watching baseball, Italian food.*
- Make a list of all the possibilities on the board.

3. Aim: to practice reading for specific information.
- Explain to the students that they will probably not know every single word they see printed in the advertisements, but they should scan the texts to find events for the people described.

> **Answers**
> jazz music – Charles Neville
> Chinese food – The Lotus Flower
> ballet – Los Angeles Chamber Ballet
> movies – Universal City Odeon
> magazines – Onbeat Magazine

4. Aim: to practice reading for specific information.
- Ask the students to complete the chart. There may not be information given for all the events.

Event	Los Angeles Chamber Ballet	Charles Neville	Universal City Cineplex Odeon	Onbeat	The Lotus Flower
Type	Ballet	Jazz Bistro	Movie	Magazine	Chinese Restaurant
Date days	March 13–17	September 12–14	-	-	-
Time	8:30 P.M.	9:00 P.M.	see advert	-	5–11 P.M.
Place	Wiltern Theater	Snug Café	-	-	4615 Beach Blvd.
Other details	Romeo and Juliet $14–$47	$22/$14	The English Patient, Twintown, Space Jam, 101 Dalmations	Information about what to do in your free time	Open 7 days a week

LISTENING

1. Aim: to practice listening for specific information.
- This activity is intended to make the students listen very carefully to the conversation. It is hoped that the language in the conversation is graded to the students' present level of comprehension.

- 🔊 Play the tape and ask the students to underline anything which is different from what they hear.

> **Answers**
> **A** Do you like rock music?
> **B** No, I don't. I hate it.
> **A** What kind of music do you like? Do you like jazz?
> **B** Yes, I do. I love it.
> **A** Who's your favorite musician?
> **B** Miles Davis. He's awesome!
> **A** I don't like him that much. I don't like jazz.
> **B** Oh, I love it. What about you? Who's your favorite singer?
> **A** I like classical music. My favorite singer is Luciano Pavarotti. Do you like classical music?
> **B** It's all right.

2. Aim: to check comprehension.
- Ask the students to correct the written conversation with what they heard.

- 🔊 Play the tape so students can check their answers.

3. Aim: to practice speaking.
- Ask the students to act out the conversation. When they have done it two or three times with different students, ask two or three pairs to act it for the whole class.

GRAMMAR AND FUNCTIONS

1. **Aim: to present subject and object pronouns.**

● Ask the students to read the information in the grammar box and then to do the activities.

● Ask the students to look at the grammar box and to count the number of pronouns which have the same form as subject and object pronouns.

> **Answer**
> The following pronouns are the same as subject and object: *you, it*

2. **Aim: to focus on the language for talking about likes and dislikes.**

● Ask the students to complete the conversation. You may like to do this orally with the whole class.

> **Answers**
> A Do you like the actress Demi Moore?
> B Yes, I do. She's great. What about you? Do you like her?
> A No, I don't. I don't like her at all.
> B Who's your favorite film star?
> A I like Jodie Foster.

● Ask the students to work in pairs and to act out the conversation once as it stands and once replacing the names with their own favorite actors and actresses.

3. **Aim: to practice using subject and object pronouns.**

● Ask the students to do this activity orally in pairs.

> **Answers**
> 1. her 2. them 3. We 4. him

● As a follow-up activity you may like to ask the students to think about their favorite well-known people and places, for example, favorite movie star, singer, sports personality, politician, club, TV show, movie, or restaurant. They should make a list.

● Then ask the students to ask and say who their favorite people and places are.

● Find out who are the most popular people and what are the most popular places among the students.

LISTENING AND WRITING

1. **Aim: to prepare for listening.**

● Ask the students to look at the penfriend advertisements and to see if there is anyone who has similar interests.

2. **Aim: to practice listening for main ideas.**

● 🖭 Play the tape. Ask the students to listen to four people and to focus on what they like doing.

> **Answer**
> **John:** likes sports – football, tennis, skiing, rock music
> **Kate:** likes sports – skiing, ice-skating, going to movies
> **Kenneth:** likes computer games, water sports, swimming, water polo, dancing
> **Susie:** likes going to the beach, dancing, swimming, reading, going to the theater

● Ask the students to decide on a suitable penfriend for Octavio, Kevin, and Nancy.

> **Possible Answers**
> Kenneth and Octavio
> Kate and Kevin
> John and Nancy

3. **Aim: to practice writing.**

● Ask the students to write similar paragraphs about themselves, modeled on the ads.

● Put the ads on the wall. Are there any possible penfriends that can be matched in your class?

Progress Check 6–10

GENERAL COMMENTS

You can work through this Progress Check in the order shown, or concentrate on areas which have caused difficulty in Lessons 6 to 10. You can also let the students choose the activities they would like or feel the need to do.

VOCABULARY

1. Aim: to present the parts of speech.
- Use the students' own language, if you can, to illustrate what a noun, verb, adjective, pronoun, and preposition are. Does their language have similar words or are some parts of speech contained within suffixes, inflexions, or in some other way?

- Ask the students to decide what part of speech the words are.

Answers
breakfast (n), from (prep), husband (n), on (prep), read (v), football (n), restaurant (n), to (prep), living room (n), see (v), phone (n, v), red (adj), beautiful (adj), they (pr)

2. Aim: to focus on collocations.
- Remind the students that a collocation is when two words go together. They did some work on this in Lesson 9.

Possible Answers

go to bed	have dinner
watch a video	listen to a concert
play guitar	play tennis

GRAMMAR

1. Aim: to review plural forms.

Answers
1. children
2. boys
3. men
4. women
5. brothers
6. families

2. Aim: to review the use of the apostrophe.

Answers
I don't have any sisters, but I have two brothers. My brothers' names are Tom and Henry. Tom's a doctor and Henry's a teacher. Tom's married and his wife's name is Jean. They have two children. Henry isn't married but he has a girlfriend. Her name's Linda.

3. Aim: to review word order.

Answers
1. In the United States businesses close at five thirty.
2. I get up at seven o'clock.
3. In Canada children start school at eight.
4. In the United States people start work at nine.
5. In Japan they have dinner at six.
6. We go to bed at eleven in the evening.

4. Aim: to review telling the time and talking about daily routines.
- Ask the students to answer the questions describing their own daily routines.

5. Aim: to review third person singular endings.

Answers
1. does
2. likes
3. goes
4. makes
5. plays
6. eats
7. watches
8. learns

6. Aim: to review *there is/are*.

Answers
1. Yes, there is.
2. Yes, there are.
3. Yes, there is.
4. Yes, there are.
5. Yes, there is.
6. Yes, there are.

7. Aim: to review *some* and *any*.

Answers
1. some
2. any
3. some
4. any
5. any
6. some

8. Aim: to review subject and object pronouns.

Answers
1. it   2. We   3. her   4. I   5. them   6. me

SOUNDS

1. Aim: to practice the /s/ and /z/ endings for plurals.
● ▭ Play the tape so students can check their answers.

Answers
/s/: drinks, journalists, desks, sports
/z/: chairs, computers, pens, sons, schools

2. Aim: to focus on tone of voice.
● Say one or two of the sentences in an interested, lively way, and then in a dull, bored-sounding way.

● Ask one or two students to read out the sentences in an interested and a bored way.

● ▭ Play the tape and ask the students to say if the speaker sounds interested or bored.

Answers
1. interested   2. bored   3. interested
4. bored   5. interested   6. bored

READING AND SPEAKING

1. Aim: to practice reading for main ideas; to compare cultures.
● The passage describes some life events and at what age they happen in the United States. Once again, this is an opportunity for the students to compare their culture with others.

● Ask them to decide which ones are true for their country. Are there any which surprise them?

2. Aim: to practice speaking; to compare cultures.
● Ask the students to work in pairs and to talk about the age they do things in their countries.

● You may like to ask one or two pairs of students to talk in front of the whole class about the age they do things.

11

GENERAL COMMENTS

Adverbs

It is quite complex to describe the position of adverbs in a sentence, and for the sake of simplicity, this lesson focuses on the most general rules. Students will have more information and practice in placing adverbs in the right position in *Move Up* Intermediate.

Cross-cultural Comparison

You will find small differences in the daily routines of the students in your class even if they come from the same macro-culture. These differences can be just as usefully explored as the larger differences between people of different cultures. Remember that culture can involve gender, age, socio-professional status, and religion, as well as geographical origin and background.

READING

1. Aim: to prepare for reading.

● Ask the students if they have or watch breakfast TV in their countries. Find out how many students watch breakfast TV. Ask them what sort of shows there are.

● Tell the students that Katie Lunden is a breakfast TV presenter. Ask them to predict what time her day begins and ends.

2. Aim: to practice reading for main ideas.

● Ask the students to read the passage and find out if they guessed correctly in 1.

● Try to discourage them from asking about too many vocabulary items. If you explain every word they don't understand, you may increase their vocabulary but you won't develop their ability to deal with reading passages.

> **Answers**
> She gets up at three thirty and goes to bed at eight thirty in the evening.

3. Aim: to practice understanding text organization.

● This activity type is used several times in the *Move Up* series. It is designed to help the students focus on the logical order in which information occurs in a passage, and it is also a motivating activity type. Even if the students don't enjoy the text, it is to be hoped that they will enjoy the task.

> **Answers**
> Sentence a goes after ...*and finishes at nine o'clock.*
> Sentence b goes after ...*I leave the studio at a quarter after ten.*
> Sentence c goes after ...*and I cook dinner.*

4. Aim: to practice reading for specific information; to practice writing questions.

● This activity will encourage the students to think carefully about what was actually said during the interview with Katie Lunden.

● Ask the students to write the questions the journalist asked.

> **Possible Answers**
> What time does your working day start?
> What time do you leave the house?
> What time do you get to the studio?
> What time does the show start and finish?
> What do you do after the show?
> What time do you get home?
> What do you do in the afternoon?
> What time does your husband get home?
> What do you do in the evening?
> When do you have dinner?
> When do you go to bed?
> What do you do on the weekend?

● You may like to ask some students to write the questions for the first half of the passage, and some for the second half.

● Students from each half should ask and answer the questions.

GRAMMAR

1. Aim: to focus on negatives and -s endings.
- Ask the students to read the information in the grammar box and then to do the activities.
- Ask the students to count the number of negatives and -s endings.

> **Answers**
> **Negatives:** 2 *(don't go out, don't get up)*
> **-s endings:** 6 *(starts, arrives, starts, finishes, helps, gets)*

2. Aim: to focus on the position of adverbs.
- Ask the students to put the adverbs in the right position. You may like to do this orally with the whole class, but it may be worthwhile for students to write the sentences in full afterwards.

> **Answers**
> 1. I **usually** get up at seven o'clock.
> 2. I **never** do the laundry.
> 3. She **often** has a drink with friends.
> 4. He **sometimes** goes to bed at eleven o'clock.
> 5. I'm **usually** asleep at midnight.
> 6. I'm **never** up at five o'clock in the morning.

3. Aim: to focus on prepositions of time.
- Ask the students to do this activity on their own and then to check it in pairs.

> **Answers**
> 1. from, to   2. at   3. at   4. on   5. on   6. on

VOCABULARY AND SPEAKING

1. Aim: to present the words and expressions in the vocabulary box.
- Ask the students to look at the activities in the box. Make sure everyone understands what the words and expressions mean.
- Ask the students to underline the activities they do every day.

2. Aim: to practice using the expressions in the vocabulary box; to practice speaking.
- Ask the students to work in pairs and to ask and say which activities they do every day.
- Write the activities on the board and count the number of students who do the activities every day.

LISTENING AND WRITING

1. Aim: to prepare for listening.
- Ask the students to look at the list of activities and to say which ones they do every day.
- As they have just done a similar activity with the expressions in the vocabulary box, this activity should be completed quickly.

2. Aim: to listen for main ideas.
- 🔊 Ask the students to listen to Sam and to check the activities he does in a typical day.

3. Aim: to check comprehension; to practice using adverbs of frequency.
- Ask the students to work in pairs and to check their answers.

	Sam
go to a club	✓ always
go to a party	✓ always
do some work	
have breakfast	✓ usually
have lunch	✓ usually
go to bed	✓
have dinner at a restaurant	✓ usually
go to a concert	✓ sometimes
meet friends	✓ always
play hockey	✓ often
call a friend	✓ always on Sundays
go to work/school	

4. Aim: to practice writing; to practice using *then, after that, after* + time of day.
- Ask the students to write a magazine article about a typical day in their lives. Make sure they follow the guided writing instructions.
- You may like to ask the students to do this activity for homework.

12

GENERAL COMMENTS

The Article

For speakers of many languages, especially for those whose mother tongue has no article system, the article system in English is very complex. This lesson focuses on a few of the most useful rules about the definite, indefinite, and the so-called zero article. Many teachers will assume that it's better to cover the use of articles on an *ad hoc* basis, relying on exposure and acquisition, rather than formal teaching. There is much in favor of this approach, but it is felt that a simple lesson such as this is useful in drawing attention to the issue and raising some of the difficulties.

VOCABULARY AND READING

1. Aim: to present the words in the vocabulary box.
- Ask the students to look at the pictures and to say what kinds of transport they can see. This may be a good opportunity to reactivate passive knowledge of the words to describe kinds of transport.

> **Answer**
> plane

- Explain that the Communication Activity contains pictures showing the other kinds of transport.

2. Aim: to present the words in the vocabulary box.
- The words in the box are the places which are linked with the kinds of transport in 1. You may like to explain that *garage* has two meanings: a building next to a house, where people park their cars; and a place where people take cars to be fixed by mechanics.

- Ask the students to match the places and the kinds of transport.

> **Answer**
> **station:** train, subway, bus
> **airport:** helicopter, plane
> **garage:** car, bicycle
> **bus stop:** bus
> **port:** ferry

3. Aim: to present the words in the vocabulary box.
- This is the last of the three activities focusing on collocations in the word field of transport.

- Ask the students to match the verbs with the means of transport.

> **Answers**
> **drive:** a car, a bus
> **ride:** a bicycle, a bus, the subway
> **take:** a bus, a train, a plane, a ferry, the subway
> **fly:** a plane, a helicopter

4. Aim: to check comprehension.
- Explain that there is one word in each group of words which doesn't belong. Ask the students to decide which word it is.

> **Answers**
> 1. train   2. bike   3. drive   4. airport

- Can the students explain why these words don't belong?

5. Aim: to present the words in the vocabulary box.
- Write these adjectives on the board.
  cheap far fast

- Ask the students to match the adjectives and their opposites.

> **Answers**
> cheap – expensive, far – near,
> fast – slow, rich – poor
> The word without an opposite is *crowded*.

6. Aim: to prepare for reading; to practice reading for main ideas.
- Ask the students how they get to work or school, and point out the expressions they can use to answer.

- Encourage the students to think about the title of the passage and to predict the answer to it.

> **Answers**
> by boat, by plane, by helicopter, and on foot

- Ask the students to read the passage quickly and see if they guessed correctly.

7. Aim: to practice reading for specific information.

● Ask the students to work in pairs and to answer the questions.

● If there's time, do this activity in writing.

> **Answers**
> 1. He lives in Seattle.
> 2. He goes by boat.
> 3. He goes to work at 7 o'clock.
> 4. He goes by plane.
> 5. It takes about thirty minutes.
> 6. On the roof of his office.
> 7. He's an accountant.

GRAMMAR AND FUNCTIONS

1. Aim: to focus on the uses of the article.

● Ask the students to read the information in the grammar box and then to do the activities.

● You may need to give the students a lot of help with this activity. It takes an inductive approach to the presentation of the uses of the article.

> **Answers**
> **Indefinite article with jobs.**
> *I'm **an** accountant.*
> **Indefinite article when you talk about something for the first time.**
> *I have **an** office in St. Louis.*
> **Definite article when you talk about something again.**
> *I park on **the** roof of the office.*
> **Definite article when there is only one.**
> *There isn't any traffic in **the** sky.*
> **No article with most lakes and countries.**
> *I go across Lake Washington.*
> **No article with certain expressions.**
> *I go by boat.*
> *I go to work on foot.*

2. Aim: to practice using the article.

● You may like to do this activity orally.

> **Answers**
> Nick Bartoli is **a** flight attendant. He works on **the** shuttle service between –Boston, –New York and –Washington D.C. He travels to Boston and Washington several times **a** week. He lives in **an** apartment in New York. **The** apartment is about thirty minutes from –J.F.K. Airport. And how does he get to –work? By –bicycle!

3. Aim: to practice talking about travel.

● Ask the students to do this activity in pairs and match the questions and answers.

● Ask the students to work in pairs and ask and answer the questions.

> **Answers**
> 1. e   2. d   3. a   4. b   5. c

SPEAKING AND WRITING

1. Aim: to practice speaking.

● Ask the students to find out how the other students get to school or work every day. They should use the questions in *Grammar and Functions* activity 3.

● Make sure they ask several students and note down their answers.

2. Aim: to practice writing.

● Ask the students to write a paragraph describing how one or two of the students get to school or work.

● You may like to ask students to do this for homework.

● Put some of the paragraphs on the wall. Make sure you include a description of every student's journey.

13

GENERAL COMMENTS

Modal Verbs

Modal verbs are presented in this lesson of *Move Up* Elementary, and in Lessons 6 (*can* to ask for permission), 8, and 11 (*should* and *shouldn't*) in Book B. There is a brief explanation of the features of modal verbs in the *Grammar Review*. You may decide that it is not appropriate at this level to use the term *modal verb*, but to refer to *can* and *should* simply as verbs which are exceptional in their form (no -*s* ending in the third person singular), and which are followed by another verb.

VOCABULARY AND READING

1. Aim: to present the words in the vocabulary box.
- There has already been some collocation work in earlier lessons. This activity focuses once again on words which go together. Write the verbs in the box on the board, and say them out loud. Ask the students to suggest words and expressions which go with the verbs.

- Ask the students to suggest other words and expressions which go with the verbs.

> **Answers**
> cook a meal, do a crossword, play a muscial instrument, ride a horse, speak a foreign language, use a computer, write poetry

2. Aim: to present the words in the vocabulary box.
- These verbs can be used intransitively, that is, without an object. Ask the students to match them with the pictures.

> **Answers**
> **picture a:** type
> **picture b:** swim
> **picture c:** ski
> **picture d:** draw

3. Aim: to practice using the new vocabulary; to practice reading and reacting to a text.
- Ask the students to read the questionnaire and to put either *yes* or *no* by the things which they can do.

4. Aim: to continue the reading practice.
- The fact that the questionnaire is in the second person and that there is a scoring system should ensure that the students' motivation is engaged.

- Ask the students to add up their *yes* answers and to turn to the Communication Activity. Of course, they shouldn't take the analysis of their score too seriously!

GRAMMAR

1. Aim: to practice short questions and answers with *can*.

● Ask the students to read the information in the grammar box and then to do the activities.

● Ask the students to do this activity orally in pairs.

● Check the answers with the whole class.

Answers
1. Can you swim? Yes, I can.
2. I can drive, but I can't cook.
3. I can't ski. I can't, either.
4. I can draw. I can, too.
5. Can you do crosswords? No, I can't.
6. I can't drive. I can't, either.

2. Aim: to practice using the target structures.

● Ask the students to do this activity on their own.

● Ask the students to work in pairs and to check their answers by acting out the conversation.

● 🔲 Play the tape and ask the students to check their answers.

Answers
1. d   2. c   3. a   4. b

JO	What can you do?
PAT	(1) I can run 100 yards in 15 seconds and I can use a computer.
JO	I can, too.
PAT	(2) But I can't cook very well.
JO	I can't either. But I can speak a foreign language.
PAT	(3) What language can you speak?
JO	Spanish. Can you speak Spanish?
PAT	(4) No, I can't.

3. Aim: to practice speaking.

● Ask the students to work in new pairs and to act out the conversation.

● Ask one or two pairs to act out the conversation to the whole class.

4. Aim: to practice speaking.

● Ask the students to talk about their answers to the questionnaire. The conversation in activity 2 can be used as a model.

● Ask one or two pairs to act out the conversation to the whole class.

SPEAKING

1. Aim: to practice reading for main ideas; to check comprehension; to prepare for speaking and listening.

● These statements constitute a minimal amount of reading but they need to be fully understood if they are to act as a stimulus for speaking.

● Ask your students to read them and to say which sentences are illustrated.

Answers
Thin people can't swim very well.
Chickens can't fly.

2. Aim: to practice speaking.

● Ask the students to work in pairs and to discuss which ones are true.

3. Aim: to practice speaking.

● Ask the students to work in pairs. Encourage them to write statements about people in the class or people who everyone knows. They should write two true statements and one false one.

4. Aim: to practice speaking.

● Students should now exchange their statements and read the ones they have received from another pair. They should try to guess which statement is false.

14

GENERAL COMMENTS

Prepositions

It may be useful at this stage to spend a few minutes at the beginning of the lesson reviewing the prepositions the students have come across already: *to, at, in, from, under, near*. Make sure students understand that *at* and *in* are also prepositions of time as well as place.

VOCABULARY AND LISTENING

1. Aim: to present the words in the vocabulary box.
- Ask the students to give examples of stores and town facilities near their school using the vocabulary in the box. If you're teaching in a school near a shopping mall or downtown district, you may like to draw a map of the area on the board and label the stores you can find there.

- Ask the students to complete the sentences with words from the box.

> **Answers**
> 1. post office   2. parking lot   3. library
> 4. phone booth   5. grocery store   6. train station
> 7. swimming pool   8. bakery

2. Aim: to practice using the new vocabulary.
- Ask the students to work in pairs and to say where you can buy the things shown.

- Check the answers with the whole class.

> **Answers**
> 1. flower shop   2. bank   3. drugstore
> 4. grocery store   5. bar   6. bookstore

3. Aim: to practice listening for specific information.
- Explain to the students that they are going to hear four conversations in the street and that they need to mark the names of the places mentioned on the map.

- ▣ Play the tape.

> **Answers**
> The four places are: a bank, a bakery, a drugstore, a music store

GRAMMAR AND FUNCTIONS

1. Aim: to check listening comprehension; to practice using prepositions of place.
- Ask the students to read the information in the grammar and functions box and then to do the activities.

- You may need to illustrate *next to, between, on the corner of,* and *across from* with drawings on the board. If you haven't drawn a map of your own local shopping district, it may be a good idea if you quickly copy the map in the Student's Book on to the board, so you can maintain visual contact with your students.

> **Answers**
> 1. The bank is across from the movie theater, on Valley Road.
> 2. The bakery is across from the flower shop, next to the movie theater, on Valley Road.
> 3. The drugstore is across from the restaurant, on Washington Street.
> 4. The music store is on Lincoln Street.

2. Aim: to practice using prepositions of place.
- Ask the students to continue to say where the stores and other facilities are on the map.

- You can continue this activity by referring back to the map of your local shopping district.

3. Aim: to present the language for giving directions; to practice understanding text organization; to provide a model conversation.

● Ask the students to read the sentences from the conversation and to put them in the right order.

● They can check their answers in pairs.

● 🔲 Play the tape.

Answers
d   e   b   c   a

4. Aim: to practice giving directions.

● Ask the students to act out the conversations in pairs.

● When they've done this a few times with different partners, ask two or three pairs to act it out in front of the whole class.

5. Aim: to practice using prepositions of place and giving instructions.

● Ask the students to work in pairs and to follow the instructions in the Communication Activities.

● Tell the students that each pair has the same map, but has different information about the stores and town facilities marked on the map.

READING AND SPEAKING

1. Aim: to prepare for reading; to pre-teach some new words.

● This activity is designed to start the students thinking about the passage they are going to read. Find out if every town has a Main Street. If so, where is the nearest Main Street?

● You may want to check that the students understand the words given. You can explain that a *shopping mall* is an American English expression for a commercial center, with many individual shops in one huge building.

2. Aim: to practice reading for main ideas.

● Explain to the students that the passage has one central idea, and that it's important they should understand what it is. Explain that *The End of Main Street, U.S.A.?* questions whether the Main Street as a shopping center will survive for much longer.

● Ask the students to read the passage and to decide why it is the end of the Main Street.

Answer
1

● Go back over the passage and check everyone understands why this is the correct answer.

3. Aim: to practice reading for specific information.

● These questions are designed to make the students go back over the passage and read it more closely.

Answers
1. True   2. False   3. False   4. True   5. True   6. False

● Students may like to check their answers in pairs.

4. Aim: to practice speaking; to check comprehension.

● Ask the students to discuss their answers to the questions in relation to their own country.

15

GENERAL COMMENTS

Present continuous

This is the first time the present continuous is introduced in *Move Up* Elementary, although students may have come across the tense during another course. Its main use in its present sense is to stress the temporary or ongoing nature of what is being described, as opposed to something which is finished or permanent.

LISTENING

1. Aim: to present the use of the present continuous; to prepare for listening.
- The choice of context and material is designed to reflect the principal use of the present continuous: to say what is happening at the moment.

- Ask the students if they have ever been in an airplane and if so, if they can remember some of the announcements made during the flight.

- Ask the students to read the passage and decide when it is taking place.

> **Answer**
> during the flight

2. Aim: to practice listening for specific information.
- 🔲 This activity involves some careful listening. Play the tape and ask the students to underline anything in the passage which is different from what they hear.

> **Answers**
> Ladies and gentlemen, this is the captain speaking. I hope you're enjoying your flight to San Fransisco this morning. At the moment, we're passing over the city of Portland, Oregon. If you're sitting on the right-hand side of the aircraft, you can see the Oregon coast from the windows. We're flying at 30,000 feet and we're traveling at a speed of 500 m.p.h. You'll be glad to hear that the weather in San Francisco this morning is perfect. It is sunny and warm, and the temperature is 65°. I hope you enjoy the rest of your flight, and thank you for flying Northwest Airlines today.

3. Aim: to check comprehension.
- Ask the students to check their answers in pairs. They should change the reading passage to what they've heard on the tape.

- You may like to ask one or two students to read out their corrected versions.

4. Aim: to provide an opportunity for a second listening.
- 🔲 Play the tape again and ask the students to check their version.

- As far as you, the teacher, are concerned, it doesn't matter if the students' versions are not completely accurate. The process of listening, underlining differences, and checking is more important than the final result. However, the challenge to the students to get a correct version will be a powerful motivating force.

GRAMMAR

1. Aim: to focus on the form of the present continuous.
- Ask the students to read the information in the grammar box and then to do the activities.

- Ask the students to complete the sentences. You may want to do this orally with the whole class.

> **Answers**
> 1. is 2. flying 3. aren't, flying 4. are 5. isn't, is

2. Aim: to practice using the present continuous.
- Ask the students to listen and decide what the situation is. Emphasize that they do not have to understand every single word. Even if the language is difficult, there will still be something which is comprehensible to them, and in this case, it should be the situation.

> **Answers**
> 1. in a restaurant
> 2. at a produce market
> 3. on a bus

3. Aim: to practice using the present continuous.
- Ask the students to say what the people are doing in the situations they heard.

> **Answers**
> 1. They're having a meal.
> 2. They're buying food./They're going shopping.
> 3. They're going to work.

VOCABULARY AND SPEAKING

1. **Aim: to present the words in the vocabulary box.**

● Some languages and cultures do not use the compass points as frequently as English speakers. Find out if your students come from a culture where they use them to describe, for example, different districts in a city, or different regions of their country.

● Ask the students to label the compass with the words for compass points.

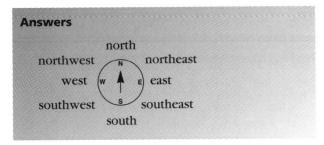

> **Answers**
>
> northwest   north   northeast
>
> west   east
>
> southwest   southeast
>
> south

2. **Aim: to practice using the new vocabulary.**

● Ask the students to describe the location of various places, including the capital city, using the compass points.

3. **Aim: to practice using the new vocabulary; to present the words and expressions in the vocabulary box.**

● Ask the students to describe the location of any of the places mentioned. If they don't know of these places, choose other places which they do know.

● Ask the students to use the words and expressions to describe the town they're in at the moment.

4. **Aim: to practice using the new vocabulary.**

● Ask the students to work in pairs and to practice describing various places.

READING AND WRITING

1. **Aim: to practice reading for specific information; to prepare for writing; to practice using the present continuous.**

● Find out who sends postcards when they're away from home, and to whom. How many are there in the class?

● Ask the students to read the postcard and to answer the questions.

> **Answers**
> 1. Janet
> 2. in a hotel in the mountains
> 3. in the hotel in the picture
> 4. to Becky Graham
> 5. yes, they are.

2. **Aim: to practice speaking; to check comprehension.**

● Ask the students to work in pairs and to check their answers.

3. **Aim: to practice writing.**

● Ask the students to use the postcard as a model, to follow the instructions and to write a postcard to a friend. They can either invent a vacation location or they can honestly describe where they are and what they're doing at the moment.

● You may like to ask the students to do this activity for homework.

Progress Check 11–15

GENERAL COMMENTS

You can work through this Progress Check in the order shown, or concentrate on areas which have caused difficulty in Lessons 11 to 15. You can also let the students choose the activities they would like or feel the need to do.

VOCABULARY

1. **Aim: to focus on international words.**
- This activity is designed to show the students that they have learned a great deal of vocabulary outside the classroom and without necessarily having realized it.
- Spend some time drawing the students' attention to the number of words which are the same in English and in their language.

2. **Aim: to focus on international words.**
- Ask the students to decide what type of words the international words are.

> **Answers**
> Pepsi, Toyota – brand names
> secretary – jobs
> pasta – food
> volleyball – sports

3. **Aim: to focus on loan words in English.**
- It may be that there are many English words in the students' language. This activity is to show that there are many words in English borrowed from other languages.
- Ask the students to say if the words are in their language, and where they come from.

> **Answers**
> siesta – Spanish, concerto – Italian,
> spaghetti – Italian, café – French, judo – Japanese,
> ballet – French, samba – Brazilian Portuguese,
> sauna – Finnish

4. **Aim: to present some everyday expressions.**
- It's difficult to fit these expressions into the vocabulary boxes in *Move Up*, so this opportunity is being taken to present them to the students. They should be words which the students will have come across beforehand, but which they may not have actively learned.

> **Answers**
> a. Please
> b. Pardon me?
> c. Excuse me
> d. Thank you
> e. Sorry

5. **Aim: to focus on some everyday expressions.**
- 🔊 Play the tape. The students listen and check their answers.

GRAMMAR

1. **Aim: to review articles.**

> **Answers**
> 1. a   2. no article   3. no article   4. The
> 5. The, the, the   6. no article

2. **Aim: to review the position of adverbs.**

> **Answers**
> 1. I usually get up at nine on Saturday and Sunday.
> 2. I often go out with friends on Saturday night.
> 3. I always go shopping on Saturday morning.
> 4. I sometimes go for a walk on Sunday.
> 5. I often watch the football game on TV on Monday night.
> 6. I usually go to bed early on Sunday night.

3. **Aim: to review question forms.**

> **Answers**
> 1. What time do you get up on Saturday and Sunday?
> 2. What do you do on Saturday night?
> 3. When do you go shopping?
> 4. What do you do on Sunday?
> 5. What do you do on Monday night?
> 6. What time do you go to bed on Sunday night?

4. Aim: to review *can* and *can't*.

> **Answers**
> 1. He can't play piano.
> 2. He can drive.
> 3. He can't use a computer.
> 4. He can't type.
> 5. He can do crosswords.
> 6. He can swim.

5. Aim: to review prepositions.
● Ask the students to write true sentences describing where places are.

6. Aim: to review giving directions.
● Ask the students to give true directions to the places they described in 5.

7. Aim: to practice the present continuous.
● Ask the students to write sentences about people and what they're doing at the moment.

SOUNDS

1. Aim: to focus on the pronunciation of /ð/ and /θ/.
● These phonemes may cause particular difficulties of speakers of certain languages, such as Japanese and Korean. Ask the students to listen and repeat the words.

> **Answers**
> /ð/: this, that, the, mother
> /θ/: think, three

2. Aim: to focus on the pronunciation of /ɑ/, /æ/, and /ʌ/.
● 🔲 Ask the students to listen and repeat the words as you play the tape.

3. Aim: to focus on stressed words in questions.
● 🔲 Ask the students to listen and underline the stressed words.

● 🔲 Ask the students to say the questions out loud.

> **Answers**
> How do you get to <u>work</u>?
> How <u>long</u> does it <u>take</u>?
> Can you speak <u>English</u>?
> Do you <u>always</u> cook <u>dinner</u>?

WRITING AND SPEAKING

1. Aim: to focus on the layout of addresses.
● Do this activity with the whole class. It would be useful for you to draw the envelope on the board and to write up the features.

> **Answers**
> **title:** Mr.
> **first name:** John
> **last name:** Smith
> **street number:** E 92104
> **road or street:** Maple
> **city:** Charlotte, NC
> **zip code:** 28204
> **country:** U.S.A.

2. Aim: to practice writing addresses.
● Ask the students to write out the addresses in the correct way. Make sure they use suitable punctuation as well.

> **Answers**
> Dr. Hillary Jones
> W 34 Denver Street
> Columbus, OH 43216
>
> Mr. Michael Carey
> N 6201 Division
> Omaha, NE 55202
>
> Ms. Kelly Green
> W 6106 Golden Hill
> New Orleans, LA 62602
> U.S.A.

3. Aim: to practice writing addresses.
● Ask the students to collect addresses and to write them down.

16

GENERAL COMMENTS

Past Simple

This is the first of five lessons in which the past simple is presented. This lesson focuses on the verb *to be*. You may find it useful to restrict the students' discussion of past events to this verb alone in the affirmative and in question form. There will be many opportunities in Lessons 18 and 20 and in Book B, Lessons 1 and 2 to cover regular and irregular verbs, and negatives.

Respecting the Class

The early stages of this activity deal with some highly personal issues and demand the affective involvement of the students. For those classes who are happy to respond, the discussion will be highly motivated. For other classes, you may think it appropriate to leave out some of the questions. The students' place is, at present, in the language classroom, not on the psychiatrist's couch!

SPEAKING AND LISTENING

1. Aim: to present the past simple form of *to be*; to prepare for listening.
● Ask the students to think about when they were a child. Ask them to work alone and to think about the questions and their answers to them. It won't yet be suitable to share their answers, because there has not yet been sufficient presentation of the past simple for them to be able to do this.

2. Aim: to practice listening for main ideas.
● The speakers in this listening activity will only talk about some of the questions in activity 1. The students' task is simply to recognize the general idea of their reply and to match it with the question in 1.

● ▭ Play the tape.

Answers
Speaker 1: What was the name of your first teacher?
Speaker 2: What was your best birthday?
Speaker 3: What was on the walls on your first classroom?
Speaker 4: Who was your first friend?

● Emphasize that it isn't necessary to understand every word, only the general sense. If you explain every word, you will not help the students to develop their ability to listen to real-life English, which will usually be above their present level.

3. Aim: to check comprehension.
● Ask the students to work in pairs and to check their answers.

● At this stage, you shouldn't expect them to formulate the past simple correctly. This activity focuses on fluency. There will be many opportunities to focus on accuracy later in the lesson.

4. Aim: to prepare for speaking.
● Ask the students to answer the questions in writing. You can go around and help people with any difficult vocabulary. You can also leave out any questions which are not appropriate to the class.

GRAMMAR

1. Aim: to focus on the form of *to be* in the past simple.
● Ask the students to read the information in the grammar box and then to do the activities.

● This is an inductive activity to help the students formulate their own rules about grammar.

Answer
Two: **was** and **were**

2. Aim: to practice using the past simple of *to be*.
● This should be the first time that the students have to produce the target structure. Do this activity with three or four students in front of the whole class, and then ask them to work in pairs.

● As they do this activity, ask the students to take notes.

3. Aim: to practice using the past simple.
● Ask the students to write their partner's answers in sentences.

● You may like to ask several students to read out their answers to the whole class.

SOUNDS

Aim: to focus on the stressed and unstressed pronunciation of *was*.
● Remind the students that the pronunciation of some words is different according to whether they are stressed or not.

● ▭ Play the tape and ask the students to say if they hear /wəz/ or /wɒz/.

Answers
1. /wɒz/
2. /wɒz/
3. /wəz/
4. /wəz/
5. /wəz/
6. /wɒz/

VOCABULARY AND SPEAKING

1. **Aim: to present the words in the vocabulary box.**
- Ask the students to match the words with the drawings.

- Check the students' answers with the whole class. On the board, write the number of the drawing by the word.

Answers
a – well-behaved
b – stubborn
c – happy
d – bad-tempered
e – shy
f – serious
g – friendly
h – lazy

2. **Aim: to check comprehension.**
- Explain that there is one word in each group of words which doesn't go with the others. Ask the students to underline it. The distinction is always between the positive and negative connotation of the words.

Answers
1. disobedient 2. happy 3. well-behaved

- Ask the students if they can explain why these words don't belong.

3. **Aim: to practice using the adjectives in the vocabulary box; to practice using the past simple.**
- Ask the students to talk about what they were like as children. Emphasize that you are thinking about their character aged between five and eight years old.

4. **Aim: to practice using the adjectives in the vocabulary box; to practice using the past simple.**
- Ask the students to identify the people in the pictures.

- Then ask the students to say what they think the people in the pictures were like as children.

- Ask the students to work in groups and to continue the activity by thinking about famous people and what they were like as children.

- Ask them to write the names of these people on separate pieces of paper. You may like to have some small squares of paper ready for this activity. A4 sheets cut into eight pieces would be a suitable size.

5. **Aim: to practice speaking; to practice using the past simple; to practice using the words in the vocabulary box.**
- Ask the students to choose one of the pieces of paper and to use the adjectives in the vocabulary box to describe what the person on their piece of paper was like as a child.

6. **Aim: to practice speaking; to practice using the past simple; to practice using the words in the vocabulary box.**
- Ask the students to read out to the other students in their group the adjectives they have used to describe the person in activity 5. They should not mention the name of the person on their paper. The other students in the group must try and guess the name of the person by the adjectives used to describe him/her.

- Ask several students to read out the name and the list of adjectives they have chosen to the whole class.

WRITING

1. **Aim: to practice writing; to practice using the target vocabulary and structures.**
- This section is meant to be a light-hearted end to the lesson.

- Ask the students to write statements about themselves as children on a piece of paper. Three statements should be true and one false.

2. **Aim: to practice writing; to practice using the target vocabulary and structures.**
- Ask the students to show each other the statements and to ask questions about them. They should write the questions on the piece of paper that the statements have been written on.

3. **Aim: to practice writing; to practice using the target vocabulary and structures.**
- Ask the students to pass back the statements and to read and answer the questions. Encourage them to be as humorous or inventive as they wish.

4. **Aim: to practice writing; to practice using the target vocabulary and structures.**
- Ask the students to keep asking and answering questions until they have guessed the false statement.

17

GENERAL COMMENTS

Cultural Bias, Cross-cultural Comparison

As *Move Up* is used by teachers around the world, it may be that some of the vocabulary items taught are not the most appropriate for particular cultural contexts. The words for food in this lesson are clearly words which are suitable to describe eating habits in North America and Europe. You may find it useful to teach these items, but to supplement the vocabulary load with food items appropriate to your own culture. The cultural bias is inevitable but should be seen positively as an opportunity to provide some cross-cultural comparison.

VOCABULARY AND LISTENING

1. **Aim: to present the words in the vocabulary box.**
- Ask the students to read the list of words and to match them with the drawings.

- Check the answers with the whole class.

> **Answers**
> **The things in the picture are:** coffee, rice, tea, lamb, egg, tomato, bread, cheese, onion, carrot, potato, lettuce, banana, apple, grapes, mineral water, lemon

- Ask the students to name the food items which they can't see.

> **Answers**
> bacon and chicken

2. **Aim: to check the meaning of the new vocabulary.**
- Ask the students to categorize the food items in the box. You may also like to ask them to do the same with any other new words which you have taught in this lesson.

> **Answers**
> **meat:** bacon, beef, chicken, lamb
> **fruit:** apple, banana, grapes, lemon
> **vegetables:** carrot, lettuce, onion, potato, tomato
> **dairy products:** butter, cheese, egg
> **drink:** coffee, orange juice, tea, mineral water
> The items which are difficult to put under headings are: bread, oil, rice

- You may like to ask the students which items of food and drink they often eat or drink. This will focus on personal differences of taste and habit, as much as on cross-cultural comparison.

3. **Aim: to prepare for listening; to present countable and uncountable nouns.**
- Ask the students to read the conversation and to decide where the missing sentences go.

> **Answers**
> 1. d   2. a   3. c   4. b
>
> JEAN   OK, what do we need?
> TONY   We need some fruit and vegetables.
> JEAN   How about some oranges?
> TONY   (1) OK, and we'll get some bananas.
> JEAN   Yes, there aren't any bananas. And let's get some apples.
> TONY   OK, apples. And we don't have any onions.
> JEAN   (2) A pound of onions. That's enough. And some carrots.
> TONY   That's right, we don't have any carrots. And let's get some meat.
> JEAN   Yes, OK. You like chicken, don't you?
> TONY   (3) Yes, chicken's great. And we need some tomatoes.
> JEAN   OK. Two pounds of tomatoes. Anything else?
> TONY   (4) No. Oh, do we have any mineral water?
> JEAN   No, we need a couple of bottles of mineral water and let's get some juice. That's it.

- 🔲 Play the tape and ask the students to listen and check.

GRAMMAR

1. **Aim: to focus on the use of *some* and *any*.**
- Ask the students to read the information in the grammar box and then to do the activities.

- Ask the students to do this activity in pairs.

- Check the students' answers with the whole class.

> **Answers**
> 1. some   2. any   3. some   4. some
> 5. any   6. some   7. some   8. any

- You may like to ask the students what they ate and drank yesterday. Make a list of the food and drink on the board.

- Ask the students to work in pairs and compare what they ate and drank.

2. Aim: to present countable and uncountable nouns.

● Ask the students if they have countable and uncountable nouns in their own language.

● Ask the students to decide if the nouns in the vocabulary box are countable (C) or uncountable (U).

> **Answers**
> **Countable:** apple, banana, carrot, egg, grapes, lettuce, lemon, onion, potato, tomato
> **Uncountable:** bacon, beef, bread, butter, cheese, chicken, coffee, lamb, oil, orange juice, rice, tea, mineral water

3. Aim: to practice using the target structures; to practice speaking.

● Ask the students to act out the conversation in *Vocabulary and Listening* activity 3.

● Ask two or three pairs to act out the conversation in front of the whole class.

4. Aim: to practice using the target structures; to practice speaking.

● Ask the students to work in pairs and to make a shopping list.

● Ask the students to act out a conversation based on the one in *Vocabulary and Listening* activity 3.

SOUNDS

Aim: to focus on /s/ and /z/ endings in plurals.

● Play the tape and ask the students to listen and repeat the plurals.

> **Answers**
> /z/: apples, bananas, eggs, onions, potatoes, tomatoes
> /s/: carrots, grapes

LISTENING AND SPEAKING

1. Aim: to prepare for listening.

● Ask the students to read the statements and to say if they are true for their country.

2. Aim: to practice listening for main ideas.

● This activity provides the opportunity for some cross-cultural comparison of eating habits.

● ▣ Play the tape and ask the students to check the true statements and put a cross by the false ones.

> **Answers**
>
> | | United States |
> |---|---|
> | We eat eggs for breakfast. | ✗ |
> | There's always meat and vegetables at the main meal. | ✗ |
> | We always drink wine at lunch and dinner. | ✗ |
> | We drink coffee during the day. | ✓ |
> | We often eat potatoes with our main meal. | ✓ |
> | Many people don't eat meat. | ✓ |

3. Aim: to check comprehension; to practice speaking.

● ▣ Play the tape again and ask the students to check their answers in pairs.

● Ask the whole class to check their answers. Ask them if they think eating habits in the United States are similar to those in their countries. If they are different, can they say what the differences are?

18
GENERAL COMMENTS

Bruce Springsteen and Whitney Houston

If the students haven't heard of Bruce Springsteen and Whitney Houston explain that they are well-known in many countries as singers. Both have been chosen in an attempt to find uncontroversial figures in the world of popular music.

Jigsaw Listening

In the *Listening and Speaking* section of this lesson, there is an activity which is based on a technique known as jigsaw listening with one tape recorder. The original jigsaw listening involved three or four cassette players and a listening passage divided into three or four parts and re-recorded on to separate cassettes. This version involves just one tape recorder and a task which directs different students to answer different questions as they listen to the same cassette.

VOCABULARY AND READING

1. Aim: to present the words in the vocabulary box.
- Explain that this lesson concerns short biographies of two people. Ask the students to look at the words in the vocabulary box and to use them in sentences to describe important events in their own lives.

- You may like to give the students a few personal examples to help them.

- Ask the students to talk about the life events of a famous person in their country.

2. Aim: to pre-teach some new vocabulary.
- Most of these words occur in the biography of Bruce Springsteen. Check the students understand what they mean. If they don't, they are likely to find the passage quite difficult.

- Find out how many students have heard of Bruce Springsteen. Does anyone know his music? Does anyone like it?

3. Aim: to check the answers to 2.
- Ask the students to read the passage.

> **Answers**
> **Words in the text:** song, movie, group, award, album, children

4. Aim: to practice reading for specific information.
- Ask the students to re-read the passage. They can help each other with any difficult vocabulary, but try not to explain too many words yourself.

- Ask the students to match the two parts of the sentences.

> **Answers**
> 1. c   2. b   3. a   4. e   5. d

GRAMMAR

1. Aim: to focus on the past simple form of regular verbs.

● Ask the students to read the information in the grammar box and then to do the activities.

● Ask the students to read the passage again and to write down all the regular verbs in the past simple.

Answers
formed, learned, decided, played, started, received, divorced, married

2. Aim: to focus on the past simple form of regular verbs.

● Ask the students to decide what the past simple of these verbs is. Stress that they are regular verbs and that the past simple form is predictable.

Answers
died, stayed, looked, liked, talked, visited, wanted, finished, opened, closed, watched

3. Aim: to practice using the past simple form of regular verbs.

● Do this activity orally with the whole class.

Answers
1. visited   2. watched   3. talked
4. finished   5. stayed   6. liked

SOUNDS

1. Aim: to focus on the pronunciation of past simple endings.

● Ask the students to listen and notice the pronunciation of the endings.

● 🔲 Play the tape.

2. Aim: to practice the pronunciation of past simple endings.

● Ask the students to put the words into three columns. You may like to help them by saying the words out loud yourself once or twice, although without pausing.

● 🔲 Play the tape and ask the students to check their answers. As they listen, they should repeat the words.

Answers
/t/: finished, watched, talked
/d/: learned, closed, died, stayed
/ɪd/: started, visited, wanted

LISTENING AND SPEAKING

1. Aim: to practice listening for specific information.

● Explain to the students that they are all going to listen to the same passage, but will answer different questions.

● 🔲 Play the tape. Ask the students to work in pairs and follow the Communication Activity questions.

● There is no need to check their answers to the questions as they will have a chance to do this in activity 2.

2. Aim: to practice speaking; to check comprehension.

● The students will have listened to the same tape but will have answered different questions. The main point of the activity is in this stage, where they have information separately which will allow them to complete the chart together.

Answers
Whitney Houston
Born: New Jersey, 1963
Started singing: when she was 11, later with blues singers such as Chaka Khan and Lou Rawls.
First hit: *Whitney Houston* in 1985
Appeared in *The Bodyguard:* with Kevin Costner in 1992
Number of copies sold of first two albums: 10 million
I will always love you: 1993

3. Aim: to check comprehension.

● Ask the students to match the two parts of the sentences.

Answers
1. d   2. a   3. b   4. c   5. e

4. Aim: to practice speaking.

● Ask the students to work together and to prepare a short biography of someone famous from their own country.

● You may like to ask your students to do some research for this activity for homework.

19

GENERAL COMMENTS

Cultural Sensitivities

There are some cultures which are reluctant to talk about the physical appearance of people. Even if your students do not belong to such a culture, the subject may need to be treated sensitively. For example, words which may be perceived as unkind such as *fat* or *old* are not presented in this lesson, although you may think they are suitable to include.

VOCABULARY

1. Aim: to present the words in the vocabulary box.
- Ask the students to match the words with the pictures.
- Check everyone knows what the words mean.

> **Answers**
> **picture a:** straight, short
> **picture b:** short, curly
> **picture c:** straight, young, long
> **picture d:** tall

2. Aim: to present the words in the vocabulary box.
- The words in this box describe more subjective impressions of appearance and are therefore more difficult to illustrate. You may need to think of well-known people to illustrate the meaning of some of the words.
- Ask the students to put the adjectives under the various headings.

> **Answers**
> **height:** medium-height, small, tall, short
> **build:** thin, well-built
> **hair:** curly, dark, blond, long, short, straight
> **age:** elderly, middle-aged, old, young
> **general impression:** attractive, good-looking, pretty

3. Aim: to present the words in the vocabulary box.
- Ask the students to use the words in the box to describe people in the pictures or in the class.

> **Answers**
> **picture a, b and d:** short hair
> **picture a:** gray hair
> **picture b:** moustache, glasses

FUNCTIONS

1. Aim: to present the language of describing people.
- Ask the students to read the information in the functions box and then to do the activities.
- Explain to the students that they are going to hear someone describing the people in the pictures. Ask them to listen and decide who is being described.
- 🔲 Play the tape.

> **Answers**
> **Conversation 1:** d
> **Conversation 2:** a
> **Conversation 3:** b
> **Conversation 4:** c

2. Aim: to practice describing people.
- Ask the students to work on their own and to write a brief description of someone in the pictures.
- When they are ready, ask the students to exchange their descriptions. The other student should guess who his/her partner has described.

3. Aim: to practice describing people.
- Ask the students to work in pairs and to describe someone in their family.
- Ask two or three students to give their descriptions to the whole class.

WRITING

1. Aim: to practice describing people; to prepare for writing; to practice reading for main ideas.
- Ask the students to read the letter and to decide if Nick knows Pat.

> **Answer**
> No, he doesn't.

2. Aim: to practice describing people.

● Explain that Nick is one of the people in the pictures. Can anyone see who it is?

Answer
d

3. Aim: to practice describing people; to practice writing.

● Ask the students to write a letter describing themselves to someone they don't know.

● Make sure they use the letter in activity 1 as a model. Check that the layout is appropriate. You may like to discuss the content of each paragraph and why the writer has started a new paragraph on each occasion.

LISTENING AND SPEAKING

1. Aim: to practice speaking; to prepare for listening.

● This activity focuses on stereotypical physical appearances of people from different countries.

● Ask the students if there is any physical feature which is typical of people from their countries, such as hair color or eye color.

● Ask the students to read the statements and decide if they are true or false for people from their countries.

● Discuss the answers with the whole class.

2. Aim: to practice listening.

● ▭ Play the tape and ask the students to say if the statements are true or false for Kevin.

Answers
1. False   2. False   3. True   4. False

3. Aim: to practice speaking; to practice listening for specific information.

● Ask the students to remember what Kevin said in greater detail.

● Encourage the students to try to reconstitute as much of what Kevin said as possible.

● ▭ Play the tape for students to check their answers.

Answers
1. b   2. c   3. a   4. c

20

GENERAL COMMENTS

Cities and Countries

It is not just the names of countries in English which may be different from your students' own language. The names of cities may be different as well. This lesson begins by focusing on these differences.

Irregular Verbs

Explain to the students that the past simple form of irregular verbs has to be learned as a vocabulary item in its own right. Even though some irregular verbs follow certain patterns, there are no generative rules about these verbs—otherwise they wouldn't be irregular!

Making Your Own Recordings

If you're interested in collecting your own recorded material, especially on the topic of travel, this lesson presents a model for you to follow. Ask a colleague or a native-English speaker to talk into a microphone about a journey they have made around a continent, a country, or a region, and process the recording in the same way as the sequence of activities shown in *Vocabulary and Listening*.

SOUNDS

1. **Aim: to present the English pronunciation of some Asian towns and countries.**
● Ask the students to match the towns and the countries.

> **Answers**
> Bangkok – Thailand, Seoul – Korea, Kyoto – Japan, Kuala Lumpur – Malaysia, Taipei – Taiwan, Shanghai – China

2. **Aim: to check the pronunciation of towns and countries.**
● Check everyone knows what the English name is for their own town and country.

● You may like to do a similar activity to 1 with the English form of towns and countries in your region of the world.

VOCABULARY AND LISTENING

1. **Aim: to present the words in the vocabulary box.**
● Once again, this is an activity which focuses on words which go together. Ask the students to match the verbs and the noun phrases.

> **Possible Answers**
> buy some souvenirs, go shopping, find a cheap hotel, fly home, go to a temple, have a meal, listen to a concert, lose your wallet, make friends, read the newspaper, stay with friends, watch a parade, visit a museum, do some sightseeing, write some postcards

● There are other possible answers, but these are the ones you'll hear in the listening passage.

2. **Aim: to prepare for listening; to listen for main ideas.**
● Ask the students to look at the map of Asia and to find places they'd like to visit. Ask them to work in pairs and then ask them to tell the rest of the class where they'd like to go and why.

● 🖭 Play the tape and ask the students to follow Mary and Bill's route around Asia.

> **Answer**
> Kyoto, Seoul, Hong Kong, Bangkok, Japan, then back to New York.

3. **Aim: to check comprehension; to prepare to practice the target structures.**
● Ask the students to check the things Mary and Bill did on their tour.

● 🖭 Play the tape. Students may like to check their answers in pairs.

> **Answers**
> buy some souvenirs ☑
> eat sushi in Japan ☑
> fly home ☑
> go shopping ☑
> find a cheap hotel ☑
> visit a temple ☑
> meet some New Yorkers ☑
> make friends with local people
> go to a concert
> go to a hot spring ☑
> write some postcards
> take a boat ride ☑
> watch a parade
> lose a wallet ☑
> have a meal in a restaurant
> read a newspaper
> relax in a park
> meet the Emperor

GRAMMAR

1. **Aim: to present the past simple form of irregular verbs.**

● Ask the students to read the information in the grammar box and then to do the activities.

● You may like to do this activity orally with the whole class.

> **Answers**
> become - became, buy - bought, come - came, find - found, fly - flew, get - got, give - gave, go - went, have - had, hear - heard, leave - left, lose - lost, make - made, read - read /red/, say - said, sell - sold, send - sent, spend - spent, take - took, wake - woke, win - won, write - wrote

2. **Aim: to focus on the auxiliary in past simple questions.**

● Ask the students to complete the sentences with the correct auxiliary.

> **Answers**
> 1. Did 2. Were 3. Did 4. Was 5. Did 6. Did

3. **Aim: to focus on the past simple form of irregular verbs.**

● Ask the students to do this activity in pairs and in writing.

> **Answers**
> They went to Kyoto, and went to a lot of temples.
> They ate sushi, went to a hot spring, and went shopping.
> They went to Seoul, and met some New Yorkers.
> They did a lot of sightseeing with them.
> They went to Hong Kong and found a cheap hotel.
> They went shopping.
> They went to Bangkok.
> Mary bought some souvenirs, and Bill took a boat ride.
> Bill lost his wallet.
> They flew back to Japan and then to New York.

4. **Aim: to focus on short answers.**

● Ask the students to do this orally.

> **Answers**
> 1. Yes, he did.   2. No, they didn't.
> 3. No, they didn't. 4. No, they didn't.
> 5. Yes, they did.   6. Yes, he did.
> 7. Yes, they did.   8. No, they didn't.

SPEAKING

Aim: to practice speaking; to practice using the target structures.

● Ask the students to go around talking to other students and asking about their last vacation.

● Ask the students to write down the names of the people they find in the *Find Someone Who...* activity.

● Ask several students to report back to the class on who they found had done the things mentioned.

● You may like to ask the students to work in pairs and to talk about a vacation they had.

● They should talk about where they went, what they did, where they stayed, how long they stayed there, what the weather was like, and when they went home.

● You may like to ask the students to write a short paragraph about their vacation, using the prompts in this activity.

Progress Check 16–20

GENERAL COMMENTS

You can work through this Progress Check in the order shown, or concentrate on areas which have caused difficulty in Lessons 16 to 20. You can also let the students choose the activities they would like or feel the need to do.

VOCABULARY

1. **Aim: to help the students organize their new vocabulary and related words.**
● Remind the students that their vocabulary notebooks should not be just lists of words, but a kind of network in which the same word appears several times and is linked to words, categories or topics.

Answers
hit record – album, bread – butter,
polite – well-behaved, marriage – divorced,
attractive – good-looking, restaurant – meal,
friendly – cheerful

● Students could make their own word charts to write down new words. They should associate words in different vocabulary areas, for example, *transportation, home, time*.

● Do make sure you look at their word charts and make suggestions, but it is advisable not to give them a grade. This type of activity is designed to increase the learner's independence.

2. **Aim: to help the students organize their vocabulary by writing down other parts of speech.**
● It may be necessary to point out that a word in its different part of speech may be used in very different contexts.

Answers
Nouns formed from the following verbs:
decision, play, player, marriage, visit, visitor, start, starter
Nouns formed from the following adjectives:
happiness, laziness, attraction, youth

GRAMMAR

1. **Aim: to review *some* and *any*.**

Answers
1. some 2. any 3. some 4. any 5. some 6. any

2. **Aim: to review countable and uncountable nouns.**

Answers
Countable: carrot, egg, onion, apple, hamburger, potato
Uncountable: water, juice, beef, milk, oil, cheese, pasta

3. **Aim: to review the past simple of regular and irregular verbs.**

Answers
became, worked, decided, bought, appeared, visited, had, went, died, started, lost, landed, painted, read, invented, sent, discovered

4. **Aim: to review the language for describing people.**

Answers
1. d 2. b 3. a 4. c

5. **Aim: to review the language for describing people.**

● Ask the students to write a description of either or both of the people in the drawings. Suggest that they answer the questions in activity 4.

6. **Aim: to review the use of the auxiliaries in the past simple.**

Answers
1. Was 2. Was 3. Did 4. Were 5. Did 6. Did

7. **Aim: to review short answers in the past simple.**

Answers
1. No, he wasn't.
2. Yes, there was.
3. Yes, I did.
4. No, there weren't.
5. No, they didn't.
6. Yes, she did.

SOUNDS

1. **Aim: to focus on /ɔ/, /ɒ/ and /ɜː/.**

● It may come as a surprise to the students that the spelling of English words is only an approximate guide to their pronunciation.

● Ask the students to group the words according to the underlined sound.

Answers
There are three groups:
/ɔ/: award, divorced, morning
/ɒ/: bought, got, lost, was
/ɜː/: learned, return, served, third, word

● 🔲 Play the tape and ask the students to say the words out loud.

2. **Aim: to focus on silent letters.**

● Ask the students to say the words in this activity and to decide which letters are not pronounced.

Answers
daughter, cupboard, bought, island, comb

● 🔲 Play the tape and ask the students to say the words out loud.

3. **Aim: to focus on tone of voice.**

● 🔲 Play the tape and ask the students to listen to the sentences in *Grammar* activity 6. The students should decide if the speaker sounds bored or interested.

Answers
1. Was Milton born in Brazil? *bored*
2. Was there anything to eat at the party? *interested*
3. Did you watch the football game last night? *interested*
4. Were there a lot of people on the bus? *bored*
5. Did they arrive on time? *bored*
6. Did she get home safely? *interested*

● Ask several students to say the sentences out loud to the whole class. Make sure they sound lively and interested.

SPEAKING

Aim: to practice speaking; to review the present and past simple tenses.

● You may need to model this game yourself. If so, put the students into groups of three or four. Think of someone famous, alive or dead. Encourage the students to ask you *yes/no* questions, and make sure you give short answers. Count the number of questions each groups asks before they guess the answer. Explain that the group with the lowest number of questions wins.

● Now ask the students to play this game themselves with one student from each group thinking of a famous person and the other students asking questions. Ask them to keep score of how many questions they ask. Remember, Student A can only answer *yes* or *no*.

Communication Activities

1 Lesson 5

Speaking, activity 2

Look at this picture for 30 seconds.

Now turn back to page 11.

2 Lesson 18

Listening and Speaking, activity 1

Student A: 🔲 Listen and find out:

- where Whitney Houston was born
- who she started singing with
- how many copies of her first two albums she sold
- when she appeared in *The Bodyguard*

Now turn back to page 43.

3 Lesson 14

Grammar and Functions, activity 5

Student A: Look at the map below. Tell Student B where each place is on your map.

Now listen to Student B and mark the stores and other places he/she describes.

When you're done, show your map to your partner. Have you marked the map correctly?

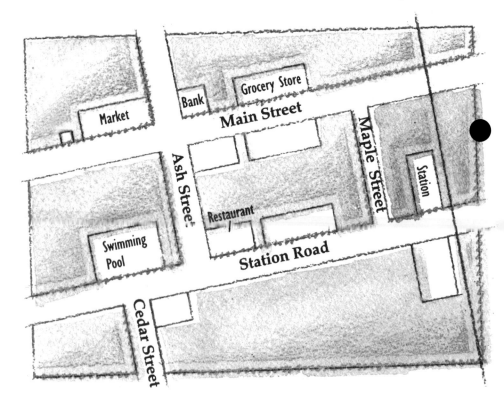

Now turn back to page 33.

4 *Lesson 2*

Vocabulary and Sounds, activity 2

Look at the pictures for different jobs and check that you know what the jobs are.

secretary

teacher

student

receptionist

farmer

5 *Lesson 12*

Vocabulary and Reading, activity 1

Look at the pictures of different means of transport and check that you know what the words mean.

train

bicycles

ferry

plane

subway

bus

car

6 *Lesson 6*

Vocabulary, activity 2

Look at the picture of Holly's family.
Did you guess correctly in activity 1?

1 Andrew, brother

2 Toni, Andrew's wife

3 David, grandfather

4 Philip, father

5 Steve, brother

6 Kate, grandmother

7 Jenny, mother

8 Holly, daughter

Now turn back to page 14.

7 *Lesson 14*

Grammar and Functions, activity 5

Student B: Listen to Student A and mark the stores and other places he/she describes. Now tell Student A where each place is on your map.

When you're done, show your map to your partner.
Have you marked the map correctly?

Now turn back to page 33.

8 *Lesson 4*

Sounds and Vocabulary, activity 2

Check your answers.

3, 13, 30, 4, 14, 40, 5, 15, 50, 6, 16, 60, 7, 17, 70, 8, 18, 80, 9, 19, 90 100

Now turn back to page 8.

9 *Lesson 18*

Listening and Speaking, activity 1

Student B: 🔊 Listen and find out:

– when Whitney Houston was born
– when she started singing
– when she had her first hit
– who she appeared with in *The Bodyguard*
– when she had a hit with *I will always love you*

Now turn back to page 43.

10 *Lesson 13*

Vocabulary and Reading, activity 4

11–15 points. Excellent! You can do it all! Way to go!

6–10 points. Good. You can do many different things. Keep trying to do more!

1–5 points. You aren't that interested in doing a lot of things. You like to specialize!

Now turn back to page 30.

Grammar Review

CONTENTS

Present simple

Form

You use the contracted form in spoken and informal written English.

Be

Affirmative	Negative
I'm (I am)	I'm not (am not)
you	you
we 're (are)	we aren't (are not)
they	they
he	he
she 's (is)	she isn't (is not)
it	it

Questions	Short answers
Am I?	Yes, I am.
	No, I'm not.
Are you/we/they?	Yes, you/we/they are.
	No, you/we/they're not.
Is he/she/it?	Yes, he/she/it is.
	No, he/she/it isn't.

Have

Affirmative	Negative
I	I
you have	you haven't (have not)
we	we
they	they
he	he
she has	she hasn't (has not)
it	it

Questions	Short answers
Have I/you/we/they?	Yes, I/you/we/they have.
	No, I/you/we/they haven't
Has he/she/it?	Yes, he/she/it has.
	No, he/she/it hasn't.

Regular verbs

Affirmative	Negative
I	I
you work	you don't (do not) work
we	we
they	they
he	he
she works	she doesn't (does not) work
it	it

Questions	Short answers
Do I/you/we/they work?	Yes, I/you/we/they do.
	No, I/you/we/they don't (do not).
Does he/she/it work?	Yes, he/she/it does.
	No, he/she/it doesn't (does not).

Question words with *is/are*

What's your name?   Where are your parents?

Question words with *does/do*

Where does he live?   What do you do?

Present simple: third person singular

You add -*s* to most verbs.
takes, gets
You add -*es* to *do, go* and verbs which end in
-*ch*, -*ss*, -*sh* and -*x*.
does, goes, watches, finishes, fixes
You drop the -*y* and add -*ies* to verbs ending in -*y*.
carries, tries

Use

You use the present simple:

- to talk about customs. (See Lesson 7.)
  In Mexico people have dinner at ten or eleven in the evening.
  In the United States people leave work at five in the afternoon.

- to talk about habits and routines. (See Lesson 9.)
  I go running every day.
  We see friends on the weekend.

- to say how often you do things. (See Lesson 11.)
  I always get up at seven o'clock.
  I sometimes go shopping in the evening.

Present continuous

Form

You form the present continuous with *be* + present participle (-*ing*). You use the contracted form in spoken and informal written English.

Affirmative	Negative
I'm (am) working	I'm not (am not) working
you	you
we 're (are) working	we aren't (are not) working
they	they
he	he
she 's (is) working	she isn't (is not) working
it	it

Questions	Short answers
Am I working?	Yes, I am.
	No, I'm not.
Are you/we/they working?	Yes, you/we/they are.
	No, you/we/they aren't.
Is he/she/it working?	Yes, he/she/it is.
	No, he/she/it isn't.

Question words

What are you doing?   Why are you laughing?

Present participle (*ing*) endings

You form the present participle of most verbs by adding -*ing*:
go – going   visit – visiting

You drop the -*e* and add -*ing* to verbs ending in -*e*.
make – making   have – having

You double the final consonant of verbs of one syllable ending in a single vowel and a consonant and add -*ing*.
get – getting   shop – shopping

You add -*ing* to verbs ending in a vowel and -*y* or -*w*.
draw – drawing   play – playing

You don't usually use these verbs in the continuous form.
believe feel hate hear know like love see smell sound taste think understand want

Use

You use the present continuous:

- to describe something that is happening now or around now. (See Lesson 15.)
  We're flying at 30,000 feet.
  She's wearing a yellow dress.

Past simple

Form

You use the contracted form in spoken and informal written English.

Be

Affirmative	Negative
I	I
he was	he wasn't (was not)
she	she
it	it
you	you
we were	we weren't (were not)
they	they

Have

Affirmative	Negative
I	I
you	you
we	we
they had	they didn't (did not) have
he	he
she	she
it	it

Regular verbs

Affirmative	Negative
I	I
you	you
we	we
they worked	they didn't (did not) work
he	he
she	she
it	it

Questions	Short answers
Did I/you/we/they work? he/she/it	Yes, I/you/we/they did. he/she/it
	No, I/you/we/they didn't. he/she/it

Question words

What did you do yesterday?   Why did you leave?

Past simple endings

You add -*ed* to most regular verbs.
walk – walked   watch – watched

You add -*d* to verbs ending in -*e*.
close – closed   continue – continued

You double the consonant and add -*ed* to verbs of one syllable ending in a single vowel and a consonant.

stop – stopped   plan – planned

You drop the *-y* and add *-ied* to verbs ending in *-y*.
study – studied   try – tried

You add *-ed* to verbs ending in a vowel + *-y*.
play – played   annoy – annoyed

Pronunciation of past simple endings

/t/ *finished, liked, walked*

/d/ *continued, lived, stayed*

/ɪd/ *decided, started, visited*

Use

You use the past simple:

● to talk about an action or event in the past that is finished.
(See Lessons 16, 18, and 20.)
What were you like as a child?
I started learning English last year.
Did they go to Hong Kong last year?

Questions

You can form questions in two ways:

● without a question word. (See Lesson 3.)
Are you American?
Was he born in Japan?
Do you have any brothers?
Did you get up late this morning?

● with a question word such as *who, what, where, when, how,* and *why.* (See Lesson 9.)
What's his job?
How old is he?
What do you do to relax?
Where were you born?

You can put a noun after *what* and *which.*
What time is it?   Which road will you take?

You can put an adjective or an adverb after *how.*
How much is it?   How long does it take by car?
How fast can you drive?

You can use *who, what,* or *which* as pronouns to ask about the subject of the sentence. You don't use *do* or *did.*
What's your first name?   Who was Agatha Christie?

You can use *who, what,* or *which* as pronouns to ask about the object of the sentence. You use *do* or *did.*
What did Agatha Christie do?   Who did she marry?

You can form more indirect, polite questions with one of the following question phrases.
Can I help you?
Could I have some water, please?
Would you like a regular or a large soda?

Imperatives

The imperative has exactly the same form as the infinitive (without *to*) and does not usually have a subject. You use the imperative:

● to give directions. (See Lesson 14.)
Go along Lincoln Street.
Turn left on Washington Street.

You use *don't* + imperative to give a negative instruction.
Don't turn right on Valley Road.

Verb patterns

There are several possible patterns after certain verbs which involve *-ing* form verbs and infinitive constructions with or without *to.*

-ing form verbs

You can put an *-ing* form verb after certain verbs.
(See Lesson 10.)
I like playing soccer on the beach.
Pete hates traveling by plane.

Remember that *would like to do something* refers to an activity at a specific time in the future.
I'd like to go to a movie next Saturday.

When you *like doing something,* this is something you enjoy all the time.
I like going to movies. I go most weekends.

to + infinitive

You can put *to* + infinitive after many verbs.
Here are some of them:
decide go have hope learn like need want
He decided to go to Mexico for a vacation.

Modal verbs

The following verbs are modal verbs.
can could should will would

Form

Modal verbs:

● have the same form for all persons.
I should go.   He should be quiet.

● don't take the auxiliary *do* in questions and negatives.
Can you use a computer?
You shouldn't be late for the meeting.

● take an infinitive without *to.*
I can type.
You should see a doctor.

Use

You use *can*:

- to talk about general ability, something you are able to do on most occasions. (See Lesson 13.)
  I can play the piano.
  I can drive a car.

You can also use *could*. *Can* is a little less formal than *could*.

You use *could*:

- to ask for something politely.
  Could I have some water, please?

- to ask people to do things
  Could you tell me your name?

- to ask for permission
  Could I try this on?

Pronouns

Subject	Object
(See Lesson 10.)	(See Lesson 10.)
I	me
you	you
he	him
she	her
it	it
we	us
they	them

Articles

There are many rules for the use of articles. Here are some of the most useful. (See Lessons 2 and 12.)

You use the indefinite article (*a/an*):

- to talk about something for the first time.
  He works in an office in Seattle.
  I get a train to work.

- with jobs.
  He's an accountant.
  He's a flight attendant.

- with certain expressions of quantity.
  I go to a movie once or twice a month.
  There are several trains a day.

You use *an* for nouns which begin with a vowel.
an accountant, an apple

You use the definite article (*the*):

- to talk about something again.
  The office is in the center of town.

- when there is only one.
  the sky
  the sun

Before vowels you pronounce *the* /ði:/.
You don't use any article:

- with certain expressions.
  by train   by plane   at work   at home

- with most countries, meals, languages.
  She often goes to Disneyland.
  She lives in Ohio.
  Let's have lunch.
  I speak Russian.

Plurals

You form the plural of most nouns with *-s*.
(See Lessons 4 and 6.)
bag – bags, book – books, key – keys

For nouns which end in *-y*, you drop *-y* and add *-ies*.
diary – diaries, baby – babies

You add *-es* to nouns which end in *-o*, *-ch*, *-ss*, *-sh*, and *-x*.
watch – watches, glass – glasses

There are some irregular plurals.
man – men, woman – women, child   children

Possessives

Possessive *'s*

You add *'s* to singular nouns to show possession.
(See Lesson 6.)
John's mother.   His teacher's book.

You add *'* to regular plural nouns.
My parents' names are Jorge and Pilar.
The boys' room.

You add *'s* to irregular plural nouns.
Their children's names are Pedro and Tomás.
The men's room.

Possessive adjectives

You can find the main uses for possessive adjectives in Lesson 2.

Form						
I	you	he	she	it	we	they
my	your	his	her	its	our	their

Expressions of quantity

Countable and uncountable nouns

Countable nouns have both a singular and a plural form. (See Lesson 17.)
a banana – bananas, a tomato – tomatoes

Uncountable nouns do not usually have a plural form.
water, juice, wine

If you talk about different kinds of uncountable nouns, they become countable.
Budweiser and Coors are both American beers.

Some and any

You usually use *some* with plural and uncountable nouns in affirmative sentences when you are not interested in the exact number. (See Lessons 8 and 17.)
We need some fruit and vegetables.

You usually use *any* with plural and uncountable nouns in negative sentences and questions. (See Lessons 8 and 17.)
We don't have any carrots.
Do we have any milk?

You use *some* in questions when you ask for, offer, or suggest something.
How about some oranges?

Adjectives

Position of adjectives

You can put an adjective in two positions. (See Lesson 4.)

- after the verb *to be*.
  The book is interesting.

- before a noun.
  It's an interesting book.

Adverbs

Position of adverbs of frequency

You usually put adverbs of frequency before the verb. (See Lesson 11.)
I always get up at seven o'clock.
I often have a drink with friends.

But you put them after the verb *to be*.
I'm never late for work.

Prepositions of time and place

in, at, on, to

You use *in*:

- with seasons and months of the year.
  in winter, in September, in March

- with places. (See Lesson 5.)
  in the classroom, in the photograph, in Ecuador

- with times of the day. (See Lesson 7.)
  in the morning, in the afternoon

You use *at*:

- with certain expressions. (See Lesson 11.)
  at school, at home, at work

- with times of the day. (See Lesson 11.)
  at night, at seven o'clock

You use *on*:

- with days and dates. (See Lesson 11.)
  on Sunday, on Monday morning, on June 15, on the weekend

You use *to*:

- with places.
  Bridget goes to Florida every month.

You use *from... to ...*:

- to express how long something lasts. (See Lesson 11.)
  The store is open from seven to nine o'clock.

Tapescripts

Lesson 5 **Listening and Vocabulary, activity 2**

Conversation 1
MAN Where's my pen?
WOMAN It's on the table, near your book.
MAN Oh, I see. Thanks.

Conversation 2
MAN Do you have a cellular phone?
WOMAN Yes, I do. It's in my bag. Here you are.
MAN Thanks.

Conversation 3
WOMAN Where's my bag?
MAN What color is it?
WOMAN It's blue.
MAN It's under your chair.
WOMAN Oh, yes. Thank you.

Lesson 7 **Reading and Listening, activity 3**

Q So, Tony, you're Australian, right?
TONY That's right.
Q And where do you come from in Australia?
TONY From Sydney.
Q Sydney! I've heard it's very beautiful there.
TONY I think it's *very* beautiful, but it is my hometown.
Q Tell me about the daily routine in Australia. What time do you get up?
TONY During the week, we get up at seven in the morning.
Q What time do children start school in the morning?
TONY It's usually about nine o'clock.
Q Nine o'clock. That's later than many countries.
TONY Yes, it is.
Q And when do they finish school?
TONY At about three in the afternoon.
Q And when do people go to work in the morning?
TONY Well, we start work at nine o'clock, so we go to work at seven thirty or eight o'clock.
Q So they start work at nine o'clock, is that right?
TONY That's right. Nine o'clock.
Q And when do you have lunch?
TONY Well, we have lunch at one o'clock. We stop work and have a sandwich usually, but our main meal is dinner, in the evening.
Q And what time do you stop work?
TONY We stop work at five in the afternoon. Actually, we leave work at five in the afternoon. We probably stop work earlier.
Q And when do you have dinner?
TONY At seven o'clock in the evening, usually. We eat outside in the yard most of the year.
Q And when do you go to bed?
TONY We go to bed at eleven or twelve at night.
Q And do you work on Saturdays and Sundays?
TONY No, we don't work on the weekend.

Lesson 8 **Listening and Writing, activity 1**

Q So Jeff, this is your home!
JEFF That's right. Do you like it?
Q I sure do! It's a very nice boat. It's so quiet here on the river.
JEFF It's sometimes noisy in the summer with the tourist boats, but in the spring and fall it's perfect.
Q How big is it?
JEFF Well, it's a special type of boat. It's called a river boat and it's thirty-five feet long and about ten feet wide.

Q Thirty-five feet! Is it difficult to drive it along the rivers?
JEFF At first it's difficult, but after a while, with practice, it's easy.
Q But I suppose with thirty-five feet, you have a lot of space.
JEFF Yes, well, we're in the living room, and there's a kitchen, a bathroom, and two bedrooms through there.
Q How many people live on the boat with you?
JEFF My wife and our baby daughter, three people in all.
Q Three of you, I see. And what sort of furniture do you have?
JEFF Well, there's a small refrigerator and a stove, several armchairs, a TV, and a shower, but there isn't room for a bath and a dishwasher. But it's very comfortable.
Q And what's the most important item for you?
JEFF I suppose it's my computer. Yes, it's my computer.

Lesson 9 **Listening and Speaking, activity 2**

Q So what do you do in your free time, Helen?
HELEN Well, I like to relax with a good book.
Q Really? You like reading, huh?
HELEN Yes, I do. I like newspapers and magazines but for me a good book is the best.
Q How about you, Chris?
CHRIS Well, I don't have much time for reading. I see my friends a lot and we go to a club every Friday and Saturday.
Q And what about during the rest of the week?
CHRIS Well, I stay home and watch TV.
Q Do you watch TV, Helen?
HELEN No, not much. There's a TV in the living room, but I only watch the news. Oh, there is one show I like—it's called *Sueños*.
Q *Sueños?* What's that?
HELEN Well, it's a very good show that teaches you Spanish. It's on public TV. I learn languages in my free time. Last year I learned French, and next year I'd like to do Russian.
Q Wow! I'm impressed! Thank you.

Lesson 10 **Listening, activity 1**

A Do you like rock music?
B No, I don't. I hate it.
A What kind of music do you like? Do you like jazz?
B Yes, I do. I love it.
A Who's your favorite musician?
B Miles Davis. He's awesome!
A I don't like him that much. I don't like jazz.
B Oh, I love it. What about you? Who's your favorite singer?
A I like classical music. My favorite singer is Luciano Pavarotti. Do you like classical music?
B It's all right.

Lesson 10 **Listening and Writing, activity 2**

JOHN Hi, I'm John, I live in Salt Lake City in Utah. I'm a college student. I like sports, football, tennis, and skiing. And my favorite music is rock music. I like the *Rolling Stones*.
KATE Hello, my name's Kate and I live in Edinburgh, in Scotland. I like winter sports like skiing and ice skating, because it gets quite cold here in Scotland. In fact, I like all sports. And I also like going to movies.
KENNETH My name's Kenneth and I live in Hong Kong. I like computer games and water sports, like swimming and water polo. I go to clubs most weekends with my friends, because I like dancing.
SUSIE My name's Susie and I'm from Melbourne in Australia. I like going to the beach and dancing, and I also like swimming. I read and go to the theater in my free time.

Lesson 11 Listening and Writing, activity 2

Q Sam, tell me about your typical day.
SAM Well, I usually get up at about noon.
Q Noon!
SAM Yes, noon.
Q But that's…
SAM Twelve o'clock, yes, that's right. Then I…
Q But what do you do?
SAM Oh, I'm a musician. But I don't have much work right now.
Q OK, so what do you do after you get up?
SAM Well, I usually have breakfast.
Q So, after breakfast…?
SAM … after breakfast, I always meet my friends and we often play hockey. And then we usually have some lunch.
Q And what do you do after lunch?
SAM Well, we sometimes go to a concert or we play some music.
Q And then what? Do you go to bed?
SAM Well, I usually have dinner at a restaurant at nine or ten in the evening if I'm hungry, and then…
Q … you go to bed?
SAM … I always go to a club or a party.
Q And when do you go home?
SAM Four or five o'clock in the morning.
Q Four or five o'clock in the morning? You do this every day?
SAM Well, not Sundays.
Q Not Sundays. What do you do on Sunday?
SAM I always stay at home and call my friends.
Q Every Sunday?
SAM Yes, most people are at home on Sunday.
Q I see. And this is a typical day?
SAM Yes, well, it's typical for me.

Lesson 14 Vocabulary and Listening, activity 3

Conversation 1

WOMAN Ah, excuse me?
MAN Yes?
WOMAN Where is the bank?
MAN There's a bank on Valley Road.
WOMAN How do I get there?
MAN Go along Washington Street, turn left on Lincoln Street. Turn right on Valley Road, and the bank is across from the movie theater.
WOMAN Thank you.

Conversation 2

WOMAN Excuse me, where's the bakery?
MAN There's a bakery next to the movie theater.
WOMAN How do I get there?
MAN Go up Lincoln Street and turn right on Valley Road. The bakery is on your left, across from the flower shop.
WOMAN Thank you.

Conversation 3

WOMAN Can I help you?
MAN Ah, yes. Where can I buy some aspirin?
WOMAN There's a drugstore on Washington Street.
MAN Oh, how do I get to Washington Street?
WOMAN Go down Wall Street and turn right on Washington Street. The drugstore is across from the restaurant.
MAN Thank you.

Conversation 4

MAN Excuse me, is there a music store near here?
WOMAN There's one on Lincoln Street.
MAN How do I get to Lincoln Street?
WOMAN Go along Washington Street. Turn right on Lincoln Street. The music store is on your left.
MAN Thank you.

Lesson 15 Listening, activity 2

CAPTAIN Ladies and gentlemen, this is the captain speaking. I hope you're enjoying your flight to San Francisco this morning. At the moment, we're passing over the city of Portland, Oregon. If you're sitting on the right-hand side of the aircraft, you can see the Oregon coast from the windows. We're flying at 30,000 feet and we're traveling at a speed of 500 m.p.h. You'll be glad to hear that the weather in San Francisco this morning is perfect. It's sunny and warm, and the temperature is 65°. I hope you enjoy the rest of your flight, and thank you for flying Northwest Airlines today.

Lesson 15 Grammar, activity 2

Conversation 1

MAN Everything all right, honey?
WOMAN Yes, everything's fine. The food is delicious.
MAN Good, I'm delighted. I love this restaurant. The chef is excellent.
WOMAN Do you come here often?
MAN Ah, well, only with very special people.
WOMAN Such as…
MAN Well, such as business clients…

Conversation 2

WOMAN Look at those oranges! Do you want to get some?
MAN 1 But we have a lot of fruit—bananas, apples, melons. We don't need oranges, too.
WOMAN And we can get some potatoes and eggs here. How much are the potatoes?
MAN 2 75 cents a pound.
WOMAN OK, I'd like five pounds.
MAN 2 Five pounds of potatoes, there you go …

Conversation 3

MAN What's happened?
WOMAN I don't know.
MAN Excuse me, what's happening?
WOMAN I don't know.
MAN Well, how long are we staying here?
WOMAN I don't know.
MAN But I'm going to work. I'm late already. What am I going to do?
WOMAN I don't know.
MAN Do you know what really annoys me?
WOMAN No.
MAN When people keep saying "I don't know."

Progress Check 11–15 Vocabulary, activity 5

Conversation 1

MAN Excuse me!
WOMAN Yes, sir. Can I help you?
MAN Yes, I'm looking for the men's department.
WOMAN It's over there!
MAN Thank you.

Conversation 2

MAN Can you carry this for me, please?
WOMAN Pardon me? I didn't hear what you said.
MAN I said can you carry this for me, please?
WOMAN Yes, of course.

Conversation 3

MAN Oh, sorry!
WOMAN That's OK.

Lesson 16 Speaking and Listening, activity 2

SPEAKER 1 Her name was Mrs. Smith. She was a tall lady, and was very old, or so it seemed. But she was a very good teacher, and she was very kind to us.
SPEAKER 2 All my friends were at my party. I remember it was a sunny day, in June, and we were all in the yard, playing together. There were tons of food and drinks and lots of games to play. Then they all sang Happy Birthday.

SPEAKER 3 There was a large map of the world on the walls of the classroom, on the one side of the board, and on the other, there was a chart to show us how to write the alphabet.

SPEAKER 4 His name was Jack, and we were very good friends. Our mothers were very good friends too, so I saw Jack nearly every day for the first three or four years of my life. Then we were at different schools, so we weren't together so much.

Lesson 17 Listening and Speaking, activity 2

Q Is it true, Lisa, that you always have eggs for breakfast?

LISA Well I guess some people do, but… People often have toast and cereal, jam, yoghurt, things like that, but not many have time to cook eggs. But if you go to a diner, you can get a big breakfast, and that usually includes eggs!

Q Do you always have meat and vegetables at the main meal?

LISA Not always, no. In any case, I don't eat meat.

Q Do people in the United States drink a lot of wine?

LISA Yes, they do, but not at every meal. They don't drink wine at lunch and dinner every day. It depends on the person… I usually have a glass of wine on the weekend.

Q What do people drink then… at mealtimes?

LISA Water, juice. Some families drink milk with their meals.

Q Do you drink a lot of coffee?

LISA Yes, people drink coffee during the day. Many people will have five or six cups of coffee a day. We usually drink it black. Other people prefer it with cream.

Q What's the main vegetable that you find at most meals?

LISA I suppose we often eat potatoes with our main meal. Potatoes are very popular. But we also eat a lot of pasta, but we don't eat pasta *and* potatoes!

Q Are there many people who don't eat meat in the United States?

LISA More and more, yes. Every restaurant will always offer several vegetarian dishes, and when people come to dinner you often check to see if there are any vegetarians.

Lesson 18 Listening and Speaking, activity 1

MAN Whitney Houston was born in New Jersey in 1963. She started singing when she was eleven years old. As a teenager she worked with rhythm and blues singers such as Chaka Khan and Lou Rawls. In 1985 she had a hit with her first album, *Whitney Houston*. She received a Grammy Award with the song *Saving all my love for you*. In 1986 she was the first pop singer to sell ten million copies of her first two albums. In 1991 she married singer Bobby Brown. In 1992 she appeared with Kevin Costner in the film *The Bodyguard*. The following year she had another hit with *I will always love you* from the film.

Lesson 19 Functions, activity 1

Conversation 1

MAN So he's going to arrive by plane from Chicago, right?

WOMAN Yes, that's right.

MAN How will I recognize him? What does he look like?

WOMAN Well, he's tall and he has short blond hair. And he's well-built.

MAN I see. How old is he?

WOMAN He's twenty-eight. I'm sure you'll recognize him.

Conversation 2

MAN I've heard so much about your mother. Tell me about her. What's she like?

WOMAN Well, she's medium-height, with short hair. She's middle-aged and she's still good-looking, I think. What else can I say? Oh, well, you can see for yourself in an hour.

MAN I am looking forward to meeting her.

Conversation 3

WOMAN 1 So you've got a new boyfriend, huh?

WOMAN 2 That's right.

WOMAN 1 What does he look like?

WOMAN 2 Oh, he's quite tall, with dark curly hair.

WOMAN 1 How old is he?

WOMAN 2 Well, he's middle-aged but he's very good-looking.

WOMAN 1 Anything else?

WOMAN 2 Oh, he has a moustache and he wears glasses.

WOMAN 1 And what does he do?

WOMAN 2 He's an accountant.

WOMAN 1 Oh.

Conversation 4

MAN So, what's the new woman at work like?

WOMAN Oh, she seems very nice. She's young. About thirty.

MAN What does she look like?

WOMAN She's very attractive, medium-height, and kind of thin with long dark hair.

MAN Hmm… When can I meet her?

WOMAN Oh, she's not your type, John.

MAN Not my type? Attractive? Thin? Long dark hair? Not my type?

WOMAN No, John.

MAN Why not?

WOMAN Well, take a look in the mirror, John.

MAN Some people think I'm very good-looking.

Lesson 19 Listening and Speaking, activity 2

Q Would you say that the Irish are tall people, Kevin?

KEVIN No, they're not very tall, I suppose we think someone is tall when they're over six feet, something like that.

Q And when does old age begin, in your opinion? How old are people when they're old?

KEVIN I suppose about sixty or seventy. No, it used to be sixty, but it's changing. No, I'd say seventy.

Q And middle age? When are people middle-aged?

KEVIN I'd say you're middle-aged when you're over forty.

Q And would you say that most people are well-built or thin or…

KEVIN Oh, it's hard to say. I suppose some of us are well-built, some of us are thin. Yes, I think it is difficult to say.

Lesson 20 Vocabulary and Listening, activity 2

MAN Hi, Mary, hi, Bill!

BILL Hello, how are you?

MAN Fine thanks, how was your trip?

MARY It was great. We had a wonderful time.

MAN Where did you go?

MARY Well, we flew to Kyoto, where we did everything the tourists usually do. We went to a lot of temples!

BILL And the weather was sunny…

MAN Great!

MARY And we ate sushi and went to a hot spring!

BILL And went shopping.

MARY Yes, we went shopping.

BILL No, *you* went shopping.

MARY OK, OK, I went shopping a lot.

BILL Then we went to Seoul, where we met some New Yorkers, and we did a lot of sightseeing with them.

MARY We had a nice time together.

BILL Then we went to Hong Kong…

MARY I've always wanted to go to Hong Kong.

BILL And we found a cheap hotel.

MAN And what did you do there?

MARY We shopped. And ate! The food there is incredible! And then we went to Bangkok.

BILL Yeah, and Mary bought some souvenirs, while I took a boat ride. And then we visited the temples. It was great.

MARY Except you lost your wallet.

BILL Yes, I lost my wallet, but someone found it and luckily it had the name of my hotel in it and I got it back.

MARY Isn't that great?

MAN Amazing.

MARY And then we flew back to Japan, and then flew home.

MAN Well, welcome home!

BILL & MARY Thank you.

Wordlist

The first number after each word shows the lesson in which the word first appears in the vocabulary box. The numbers in *italics* show the later lessons in which the word appears again.

address /əˈdres/ 3
afternoon /ˌɑːftəˈnuːn/ 7
age /eɪdʒ/ 3
airport /ˈeəpɔːt/ 12
album /ˈælbəm/ 1 -20
apple /ˈæp(ə)l/ 17
armchair /ˈɑːmˌtʃeə(r)/ 8
artist /ˈɑːtɪst/ 2
at the back /æt ðə bæk/ 8
at the front /æt ðə frʌnt/ 8
attractive /əˈtræktɪv/ 15, *19*, *16-20*,
aunt /ɑːnt/ 6
Australia /ɒˈstreɪlɪə/ 1

bacon /ˈbeɪkən/ 17
bad–tempered
     /bæd ˈtempəd/ 16
bag /bæg/ 5
bakery /ˈbeɪkərɪ/ 14
ballet /ˈbæleɪ/ 11-15
banana /bəˈnɑːnə/ 17
Bangkok /ˈbæŋkɒk/ 1, *20*
bank /bæŋk/ 14
bar /bɑː(r)/ 14
baseball /ˈbeɪsbɔːl/ 10
bath /bɑːθ/ 8
bathroom /ˈbɑːθruːm/ 8
beard /ˈbɪəd/ 19
beautiful /ˈbjuːtɪfʊl/ 4, *19*
bed /bed/ 8
bedroom /ˈbedruːm/ 8
beef /biːf/ 17
bicycle /ˈbaɪsɪk(ə)l/ 12
big /bɪg/ 15
black /blæk/ 5
blond /blɒnd/ 19
blue /bluː/ 5
book /bʊk/ 4, 5
bookshelf /ˈbʊkʃelf/ 8
bookstore /ˈbʊkstɔː/ 14
boring /ˈbɔːrɪŋ/ 15
boyfriend /ˈbɔɪfrend/ 6
Brazil /brəˈzɪl/ 1
bread /bred/ 16-20, *17*

breakfast /ˈbrekfəst/ 7
brother /ˈbrʌðə(r)/ 6
brown /braʊn/ 5
bus /bʌs/ 12
bus station /bʌs steɪʃən/ 14
bus stop /bʌs stɒp/ 12
butter /ˈbʌtə(r)/ 17, *16-20*
buy /baɪ/ 20
by bicycle /baɪ baɪsɪkəl/ 12
by boat /baɪ bəʊt/ 12
by car /baɪ kɑː(r)/ 12
by helicopter /baɪ helɪkɒptə/ 12
by plane /baɪ pleɪn/ 12

cabinet /ˈkæbɪnɪt/ 8
café /ˈkæfeɪ/ 11-15
cafeteria /ˌkæfəˈtɪərɪə/ 4
calculator /ˈkælkjʊˌleɪtə(r)/ 5
camera /ˈkæmrə/ 5
Canada /ˈkænədə/ 1
car /kɑː(r)/ 12
carrot /ˈkærət/ 17
cassette player /kəˈset pleɪə/ 4
cellular phone /ˈseljʊlə fəʊn/ 5
chair /tʃeə(r)/ 4, 8
cheap /tʃiːp/ 12
cheerful /ˈtʃɪəfʊl/ 16-20
cheese /tʃiːz/ 17
chicken /ˈtʃɪkɪn/ 17
China /ˈtʃaɪnə/ 20
Chinese food
     /tʃaɪˈniːz fuːd/ 10
classical music
     /ˈklæsɪk(ə)l ˈmjuːzɪk/ 10
classroom /ˈklɑːsrʊm/ 4
coat /kəʊt/ 5
coffee /ˈkɒfɪ/ 17
comb /kəʊm/ 5
computer /kəmˈpjuːtə(r)/ 4
concerto /kənˈtʃeətəʊ/ 11-15
cook /kʊk/ 13
cook dinner /kʊk ˈdɪnə(r)/ 11
cooking /ˈkʊkɪŋ/ 10
crowded /ˈkraʊdɪd/ 12
cupboard /ˈkʌbəd/ 8
curly /ˈkɜːlɪ/ 19
curtains /ˈkɜːt(ə)nz/ 8

dancing /ˈdɑːnsɪŋ/ 10
dark /dɑːk/ 19
daughter /ˈdɔːtə(r)/ 6
decide /dɪˈsaɪd/ 18
diary /ˈdaɪərɪ/ 5
dining room /ˈdaɪnɪŋ rʊm/ 8
dinner /ˈdɪnə(r)/ 7

dishwasher /ˈdɪʃwɒʃə(r)/ 8
disobedient /ˌdɪsəˈbiːdɪənt/ 16
divorce /dɪˈvɔːs/ 18
divorced /dɪˈvɔːsd/ 16-20
do /duː/ 13, *20*
do some work/homework
     /duː sʌm wɜːk həʊmwɜːk/ 11
do the housework
     /duː ðə ˈhaʊswɜːk/ 11
doctor /ˈdɒktə(r)/ 2
downstairs /daʊnˈsteəz/ 8
draw /drɔː/ 13
drink coffee /drɪŋk ˈkɒfɪ/ 9
drive /draɪv/ 12
drugstore /ˈdrʌgstɔː/ 14

eat an apple
     /iːt æn ˈæp(ə)l/ 9
Ecuador /ˈekwədɔː/ 1
egg /eg/ 17
eight /eɪt/ 4
eighteen /eɪˈtiːn/ 4
eighty /ˈeɪtɪ/ 4
elderly /ˈeldəlɪ/ 19
engineer /ˌendʒɪˈnɪə(r)/ 2
evening /ˈiːvnɪŋ/ 7
Excuse me
     /ɪkˈskjuːz miː/ 11-15
expensive /ɪkˈspensɪv/ 12

family room /ˈfæmɪlɪ rʊm/ 8
far /fɑː(r)/ 12
farmer /ˈfɑːmə(r)/ 2
fast /fɑːst/ 12
father /ˈfɑːðə(r)/ 6
ferry /ˈferɪ/ 12
fifteen /fɪfˈtiːn/ 4
fifty /ˈfɪftɪ/ 4
find /faɪnd/ 20
finish /ˈfɪnɪʃ/ 7
fireplace /ˈfaɪə(r) pleɪs/ 8
first name /fɜːst neɪm/ 3
five /faɪv/ 4
flower shop /ˈflaʊə ʃɒp/ 14
fly /flaɪ/ 12, *20*
football /ˈfʊtbɔːl/ 10
form /fɔːm/ 18
forty /ˈfɔːtɪ/ 4
four /fɔː(r)/ 4
fourteen /fɔːˈtiːn/ 4
fridge /frɪdʒ/ 8
friendly /ˈfrendlɪ/ 4, *16*, *16-20*

garage /ˈgærɑːdʒ/ 8, *12*
get the bus/train to work/
     school/home
     /get ðə bʌs treɪn tə wɜːk
     skuːl həʊm/ 11
get up /get ʌp/ 7
girlfriend /ˈgɜːlfrend/ 6
glasses /ˈglɑːsɪz/ 5, *19*
go /gəʊ/ 20
go running /gəʊ ˈrʌnɪŋ/ 9
go shopping /gəʊ ˈʃɒpɪŋ/ 11
go to a movie /gəʊ tuː ə
     ˈmuːvɪ/ 11
go to bed /gəʊ tə bed/ 7
go to work/school
     /gəʊ tə wɜːk skuːl/ 7
going to parties
     /ˈgəʊɪŋ tə ˈpɑːtɪz/ 10
going to the movies /ˈgəʊɪŋ tə
     ðə muːvɪz/ 10
going to the theater
     /ˈgəʊɪŋ tə ðə ˈθɪətə(r)/ 10
good /gʊd/ 4
good–looking
     /gʊd ˈlʊkɪŋ/ 19, *16-20*
grandfather /ˈgrænˌfɑːðə(r)/ 6
grandmother
     /ˈgrænˌmʌðə(r)/ 6
grapes /greɪpz/ 17
gray /greɪ/ 5
green /griːn/ 5
grocery store /ˈgrəʊsərɪ stɔː/ 14

hair /heə(r)/ 19
happy /ˈhæpɪ/ 16
hardware store /ˈhɑːdweə stɔː/
     14
have /hæv/ 20
helicopter /ˈhelɪkɒptə/ 12
hit record /hɪt ˈrekɔːd/ 16-20
husband /ˈhʌzbənd/ 6

in the mountains
     /ɪn ðə ˈmaʊntɪns/ 15
indoors /ɪnˈdɔːz/ 8
industrial /ɪnˈdʌstrɪəl/ 15
interesting /ˈɪntrəstɪŋ/ 4, *15*
international
     /ˌɪntəˈnæʃən(ə)l/ 4

Japan /dʒəˈpæn/ 1, *20*
jazz /dʒæz/ 10
job /dʒɒb/ 3
journalist /ˈdʒɜːnəlɪst/ 2

judo /ˈdʒuːdəʊ/ 11-15
keys /kiːz/ 5
kind /kaɪnd/ 4
kitchen /ˈkɪtʃɪn/ 8
Korea /kəˈriːə/ 20
Kuala Lumpur /ˈkwɑːlə ˈlumpə/ 20
Kyoto /kiːˈəʊtəʊ/ 20

lamb /læm/ 17
lamp /læmp/ 8
last name /lɑːst neɪm/ 3
lazy /ˈleɪzɪ/ 16
learn /lɜːn/ 18
lemon /ˈlemən/ 17
lettuce /ˈletɪs/ 17
library /ˈlaɪbrərɪ/ 4, 14
listen /ˈlɪs(ə)n/ 20
listen to the radio /ˈlɪs(ə)n tə θə ˈreɪdɪəʊ/ 9
lively /ˈlaɪvlɪ/ 15
living room /ˈlɪvɪŋ rʊm/ 8
long /lɒŋ/ 19
lose /luːz/ 20
lunch /lʌntʃ/ 7

magazines /ˌmægəˈziːnz/ 10
make /meɪk/ 20
Malaysia /məˈleɪʒə/ 20
market /ˈmɑːkɪt/ 14
marriage /ˈmærɪdʒ/ 16-20
married /ˈmærɪd/ 3
marry /ˈmærɪ/ 18
meal /miːl/ 16-20
medium-height /ˈmiːdɪəm haɪt/ 19
Mexico /ˈmeksɪkəʊ/ 1
middle-aged /ˈmɪd(ə)l eɪdʒd/ 19
mineral water /ˈmɪnərəl wɔːtə/ 17
modern /ˈmɒd(ə)n/ 15
morning /ˈmɔːnɪŋ/ 7
mother /ˈmʌðə(r)/ 6
movie theater /ˈmuːvɪ θɪətə(r)/ 14
music store /ˈmuːsɪk stɔː/ 14

near /nɪə(r)/ 12
New York /nuː ˈjɔːk/ 1
night /naɪt/ 7
nine /naɪn/ 4
nineteen /ˌnaɪnˈtiːn/ 4
ninety /ˈnaɪntɪ/ 4
noon /nuːn/ 7
north east /nɔːθ iːst/ 15
north west /nɔːθ west/ 15
notebook /ˈnəʊtbʊk/ 5

oil /ɔɪl/ 17
old /əʊld/ 15, 19
on an island /ɒn æn ˈaɪlənd/ 15
on foot /ɒn ˈfʊt/ 12
on the coast /ɒn ðə kəʊst/ 15
on the river /ɒn ðə ˈrɪvə(r)/ 15
one hundred /wʌn ˈhʌndrəd/ 4
onion /ˈʌnjən/ 17
orange /ˈɒrɪndʒ/ 5
orange juice /ˈɒrɪndʒ dʒuːs/ 17
outdoors /aʊtˈdɔːz/ 8
ˈpardon me /ˈpɑːd(ə)n miː/ 11-15
parking lot /ˈpɑːkɪŋ lɒt/ 4, 14
pasta /ˈpæstə/ 11-15
pen /pen/ 5
pencil /ˈpensɪl/ 5
Pepsi /ˈpepsɪ/ 11-15
phone booth /fəʊn buːθ/ 14
phone number /fəʊn ˈnʌmbə(r)/ 3
pink /pɪŋk/ 5
plane /pleɪn/ 12
play /pleɪ/ 13, 18
play guitar /pleɪ gɪtɑː/ 9
play soccer /pleɪ ˈsɒkə/ 9
Please /pliːz/ 11-15
police officer /pəˈliːs ˈɒfɪsə(r)/ 2
polite /pəˈlaɪt/ 16-20
poor /pɔː/ 12
popular /ˈpɒpjʊlə(r)/ 4
port /pɔːt/ 12
post office /pəʊst ˈɒfɪs/ 14
potato /pəˈteɪtəʊ/ 17
pretty /ˈprɪtɪ/ 19
purple /ˈpɜːp(ə)l/ 5

read /riːd/ 20
read a newspaper /riːd aɪ ˈnjuːsˌpeɪpə(r)/ 9
receive /rɪˈsiːv/ 18
reception desk /rɪˈsepʃ(ə)n desk/ 4
receptionist /rɪˈsepʃənɪst/ 2
red /red/ 5
restaurant /ˈrestəˌrɒnt/ 14, 16-20
rice /raɪs/ 17
rich /rɪtʃ/ 12
ride /raɪd/ 12, 13
ring /rɪŋ/ 5
rock music /rɒk ˈmjuːzɪk/ 10
rug /rʌg/ 8

samba /ˈsæmbə/ 11-15
sauna /ˈsɔːnə/ 11-15
secretary /ˈsekrɪtərɪ/ 2, 11-15
see friends /siː frendz/ 11
Seoul /ˈsɪəʊl/ 20
serious /ˈsɪərɪəs/ 16
seven /ˈsev(ə)n/ 4
seventeen /ˌsevənˈtiːn/ 4
seventy /ˈsevntɪ/ 4
Shanghai /ˈʃæŋhaɪ/ 20
short /ʃɔːt/ 19
shower /ˈʃʊə(r)/ 8
shy /ʃaɪ/ 16
siesta /sɪˈestə/ 11-15
sink /sɪŋk/ 8
sister /ˈsɪstə(r)/ 6
six /sɪks/ 4
sixteen /ˌsɪksˈtiːn/ 4
sixty /ˈsɪkstɪ/ 4
ski /skiː/ 13
slow /sləʊ/ 12
small /smɔːl/ 12, 15, 19
sofa /ˈsəʊfə/ 8
son /sʌn/ 6
Sorry /ˈsɒrɪ/ 11-15
south east /saʊθ iːst/ 15
south west /saʊθ west/ 15
spaghetti /spəˈgetɪ/ 11-15
speak /spiːk/ 13
start /stɑːt/ 7, 18
station /ˈsteɪʃ(ə)n/ 12
stay /steɪ/ 20
stove /stəʊv/ 8
straight /streɪt/ 19
stubborn /ˈstʌbən/ 16
student /ˈstjuːd(ə)nt/ 2
study room /ˈstʌdɪ rʊm/ 4
subway /ˈsʌbweɪ/ 12
swim /swɪm/ 13
swimming /ˈswɪmɪŋ/ 10
swimming pool /ˈswɪmɪŋ puːl/ 14
Sydney /ˈsɪdnɪ/ 1

table /ˈteɪb(ə)l/ 4, 8
Taipei /taɪpeɪ/ 20
Taiwan /taɪwɑːn/ 20
take /teɪk/ 12
take a shower /teɪk ə ʃaʊə/ 9
tall /tɔːl/ 19
tea /tiː/ 17
teacher /ˈtiːtʃə(r)/ 2
Thailand /ˈtaɪlænd/ 1, 20
Thank you /θæŋk juː/ 11-15
the United States /ðə juˈnaɪtɪd steɪts/ 1
thin /θɪn/ 19
thirteen /θɜːˈtiːn/ 4

thirty /ˈθɜːtɪ/ 4
three /θriː/ 4
toilet /ˈtɔɪlɪt/ 8
Tokyo /təʊˈkɪəʊ/ 1
tomato /təˈmɑːtəʊ/ 17
Toyota /tɔrəʊtə/ 11-15
train /treɪn/ 12
train station /treɪn steɪʃən/ 14
TV /tiː viː/ 8
type /taɪp/ 13

ugly /ˈʌglɪ/ 15
uncle /ˈʌŋk(ə)l/ 6
upstairs /ʌpˈsteəz/ 8
use /juːz/ 13

visit /ˈvɪzɪt/ 20
volleyball /ˈvɒlɪbɔːl/ 11-15

waiter /ˈweɪtə(r)/ 2
walkman /ˈwɔːkmən/ 5
wallet /ˈwɒlɪt/ 5
wash the dishes /wɒʃ ðə ˈdɪʃəs/ 11
watch /wɒtʃ/ 5, 20
watch a baseball game /wɒtʃ ə ˈbeɪsbɔːl geɪm/ 9
watching sports /ˈwɒtʃɪŋ spɔːts/ 10
weekend /ˈwiːkend/ 7
well-behaved /wel bɪˈheɪvd/ 16, 16-20
well-built /wel bɪlt/ 19
white /waɪt/ 5
wife /waɪf/ 6
wonderful /ˈwʌndəfʊl/ 15
work /wɜːk/ 7
write /raɪt/ 13, 20

yard /jɑːd/ 8
yellow /ˈjeləʊ/ 5
young /jʌŋ/ 19

Progress Test 1 Lessons 1–10

SECTION 1: VOCABULARY (30 points)

1. a. Underline the word which doesn't belong and leave a group of three related words. (10 points)

  b. Add one other word to the groups of words. (10 points)

Example: her my our <u>they</u> *their*

1. French Canada Hungary Thailand _____

2. journalist secretary taxi waiter _____

3. eight number seventeen thirty _____

4. friendly interesting kind person _____

5. beautiful orange purple yellow _____

6. aunt daughter family brother _____

7. bedroom home kitchen family room

   _____

8. bed books chair cupboard _____

9. computer television upstairs video

   _____

10. babies men people woman _____

2. Complete these sentences with ten different verbs. (10 points)

Example: I *read* a newspaper every morning.

1. I _____ with my husband in Vermont.

2. I _____ in a school. I'm a teacher.

3. I _____ up at seven in the morning.

4. I _____ to school. Our house is near the school.

5. I _____ work at four o'clock in the afternoon.

6. My husband and I _____ dinner at eight o'clock.

7. Then I _____ television.

8. I _____ to bed at eleven o'clock.

9. I _____ cereal for breakfast.

10. I _____ tennis with my husband.

© Macmillan Publishers Limited 1998.

Progress Test 1 Lessons 1–10

SECTION 2: GRAMMAR (30 points)

3. a. Choose ten of these words to complete the first ten spaces in the passage. (10 points)

Example: a) does b) has c) <u>is</u>

1. a) Her b) His c) Their

2. a) from b) in c) on

3. a) a lot b) at all c) not at all

4. a) a b) an c) any

5. a) people b) peoples c) person

6. a) a b) any c) some

7. a) a b) any c) some

8. a) watch b) watches c) watching

9. a) doesn't b) hasn't c) isn't

10. a) Their b) They c) They're

b. Complete the last ten spaces with ten of your own words. (10 points)

I have a sister and a brother. My sister *is* twenty.

(1) _____ name's Barbara. She goes to

university (2) _____ San Fransisco. Barbara

likes San Fransisco. (3) _____. It is

(4) _____ beautiful city and the

(5) _____ are very nice. Barbara has a small

room in a dormitory. There's a desk, (6) _____

chairs, and a cupboard in her room. There's a mirror

but there aren't (7) _____ plants. Barbara

doesn't have a television—she doesn't like

(8) _____ it. Barbara (9) _____ married

but she has a boyfriend. (10) _____ very

happy.

My brother's name (11) _____ Bill. He's

(12) _____ artist. Bill stays (13) _____

home every day. He works in (14) _____

studio. Bill and his wife (15) _____ two

daughters. (16) _____ names are Lisa and Jane.

They (17) _____ six years old. In the United

States children start school (18) _____ six. Lisa

and Jane are at school. Lisa doesn't like school

(19) _____ much but her sister likes

(20) _____ a lot.

4. Write your own questions for these answers. (10 points)

Example: My name's Pat.
What's your name?

1. Fine, thanks.

_____

2. I'm from Boston.

_____

3. It's West 350 Hill Avenue.

_____

4. It's (602) 647-8902.

_____

5. I'm a teacher.

_____

6. I'm twenty-five.

_____

7. Yes, I am. My husband's name is Greg.

_____

8. Yes, I have three children.

_____

9. It's blue.

_____

10. It's one thirty.

_____

Progress Test 1 Lessons 1–10

SECTION 3: READING (20 points)

5. Read the passage *How Do You Relax?* about Bill and Kate and their daughter, Sally. Complete the sentences. (10 points)

Example: __*Bill*__ likes watching football.

1. _____ likes playing sports.

2. _____ like going to movies.

3. _____ likes pop music.

4. _____ like rock music.

5. _____ likes seeing friends.

6. Answer the questions. (10 points)

Example: Who does Bill live with?
He lives with his wife.

1. Where does Bill's wife watch TV?

_____

2. When does Sally go to a club?

_____

3. Why does Kate get some Chinese food?

_____

4. What does Bill do on the weekend?

_____

5. Who does Kate go to movies with?

_____

HOW DO YOU RELAX?

I like football. I play once a week, on the weekend. I like watching it on television, too. My wife, Kate, and I have two televisions. She doesn't like watching football at all. I watch football downstairs and she watches movies in our bedroom. I like rock music too—and so does Kate.
Bill

My husband and I have one daughter. We don't usually go out in the evening. Sometimes we get a video and some Chinese food—I don't like cooking. We both like movies. Once a month my sister stays with us. She stays at home with our teenage daughter, Sally, while we go to a movie. I like going to movies.
Kate

I like listening to music. I like pop music and jazz but I don't like rock. On the weekend I go to a jazz club with my friends. Branford Marsalis is my favorite musician. I like going to movies and to the theater, too.
Sally

© Macmillan Publishers Limited 1998.

Progress Test 1 Lessons 1–10

SECTION 4: WRITING (20 points)

7. Write about your home. Write about the rooms and furniture. Write 8–10 sentences. (20 points)

Progress Test 2 Lessons 11–20

SECTION 1: VOCABULARY (30 points)

1. a. Underline the word which doesn't belong and leave a group of three related words. (10 points)

b. Add one other word to the groups of words. (10 points)

Example: her my our <u>they</u> *their*

1. after always never usually _____
2. bus plane train transportation _____
3. cheap crowded fast ferry _____
4. drugstore grocery store bookstore station

   _____
5. coast north south west _____
6. beautiful boring small city _____
7. favorite quiet shy stubborn _____
8. coffee juice oil water _____
9. curly dark hair long _____
10. fly knit run swim _____

2. Complete these sentences with ten different verbs. (10 points)

Example: You can _get_ a taxi from a taxi rank.

1. I can _____ a car.
2. She can _____ crosswords.
3. I can _____ a foreign language.
4. You can _____ some flowers at the flower shop.
5. I can _____ a meal for six people.
6. You can _____ a movie at the movie theater.
7. I can _____ a horse.
8. You can _____ a book from the library.
9. I can _____ a musical instrument.
10. He can _____ a computer.

© Macmillan Publishers Limited 1998.

Progress Test 2 Lessons 11–20

SECTION 2: GRAMMAR (30 points)

3. a. Choose ten of these words to complete the first ten spaces in the conversation. (10 points)

Example: a) <u>from</u> b) of c) to

1. a) Their b) They c) They're

2. a) from b) in c) of

3. a) stay b) stayed c) staying

4. a) along b) across from c) next

5. a) has b) is c) was

6. a) be b) go c) visit

7. a) visited b) was c) went

8. a) Am b) Are c) Is

9. a) boring b) interesting c) wonderful

10. a) by b) in c) on

b. Complete the last ten spaces with ten of your own words. (10 points)

JAMIE: Look! There's a postcard _from_ Sue and Sam.

(1) _____ on vacation in Mazatlan for a

week.

CHRIS: Mazatlan? Where's Mazatlan?

JAMIE: It's in the Gulf (2) _____ Mexico. Sue

says they're (3) _____ in a hotel right

on the beach. It's (4) _____ the market.

Mazatlan's a great place. I (5) _____

there last year.

CHRIS: Did you (6) _____ swimming a lot?

JAMIE: Yes, I did. And I (7) _____ the Inca Ruins.

CHRIS: (8) _____ Sue and Sam enjoying

themselves?

JAMIE: Yes, they're having a (9) _____ time.

They went (10) _____ plane to

Mazatlan.

CHRIS: What (11) _____ we need for dinner

this evening?

JAMIE: We (12) _____ some chicken in the

fridge. Let's get (13) _____ vegetables.

CHRIS: (14) _____ about potatoes and carrots?

JAMIE: Yes, OK. And we don't have (15) _____

onions. Let's get some onions, too.

CHRIS: Let's (16) _____ to the new grocery

store.

JAMIE: Where is it?

CHRIS: It's (17) _____ South Road. It's

(18) _____ the right. It's next to the

hardware store.

JAMIE: Oh, yes. (19) _____ you have any money?

CHRIS: Yes, I went to the bank this morning and took

(20) _____ some money.

4. Write your own questions for these answers.
(10 points)

Example: My name's Pat.
What's your name?

1. I go by bus.

_____

2. It takes about fifteen minutes.

_____

3. Seventy-five cents. It's quite cheap.

_____

4. It's about three miles.

_____

5. He's six feet.

_____

6. I'm twenty-five.

_____

7. He's very nice.

_____

8. He's tall with curly hair and glasses.

_____

9. I get up at seven thirty.

_____

10. Knit? No, I can't.

_____

Progress Test 2 Lessons 11–20

SECTION 3: READING (20 points)

5. Read the passage *A Day In The Life.*
   Complete the sentences. (10 points)

   Example: She *lives* in an apartment.

   1. She takes _____ before breakfast.

   2. She drinks _____ for breakfast.

   3. She has _____ after her singing lesson.

   4. She has _____ after she gets home from
      the theater.

   5. She goes _____ at about three o'clock.

6. Are these sentences true (T) or false (F), or
   doesn't the passage say (DS)? (10 points)

   Example: Clare doesn't have any brothers. [DS]

   1. She was born in New York. ☐

   2. She gets up late. ☐

   3. She goes to the gym in the afternoon. ☐

   4. "On the Road" is at a theater in New York. ☐

   5. She drives to the theater. ☐

A DAY IN THE LIFE

Clare Smith was born in 1976, the third daughter of the actor, Charles Smith. As a child, Clare worked in television and the theater. In 1992 Clare left school to follow her acting career. She is currently appearing in the musical, "On the Road."

I live in New York. I have a small apartment in Greenwich Village. I don't get up very early—about eleven o'clock. This is because I work in the evening and go to bed late. When I get up I take a shower. Then I have breakfast—a cup of coffee, a muffin, and some fruit. After breakfast I go to the gym for about an hour. Then I have a singing lesson. After that I have lunch, usually salad or some pasta. I don't have a big lunch. I relax after lunch. I watch a good video or I sometimes go shopping. Then I go to the theater on the subway. I'm in the musical "On the Road" at the moment. I have dinner when I get home from the theater. The evening show is at seven thirty and I get home at about eleven o'clock. I have dinner at about eleven thirty. I go to bed at about two o'clock. What time do I go to sleep? Well, at about three o'clock.

© Macmillan Publishers Limited 1998.

Progress Test 2 Lessons 11–20

SECTION 4: WRITING (20 points)

7. Write about two of your friends. What are they like? What do they look like? What do they do?
    Write 8–10 sentences. (20 points)

_____

_____

_____

_____

_____

_____

_____

_____

_____

_____

_____

_____

_____

_____

_____

_____

_____

_____

_____

_____

_____

_____

_____

Answers Progress Test 1 Lessons 1–10

SECTION 1: VOCABULARY [30 points]

1. a. (10 points: 1 point for each correct answer.)

1. French	6. family
2. taxi	7. home
3. number	8. books
4. person	9. upstairs
5. beautiful	10. woman

b. (10 points: 1 point for each appropriate answer.)

1. a country, e.g. *Japan, the United States*
2. a job, e.g. *farmer, teacher*
3. a number, e.g. *four, twenty*
4. an adjective, e.g. *good, popular*
5. a color, e.g. *gray, pink*
6. a family member, e.g. *grandmother, son*
7. a room or place in the home, e.g. *dining room, living room*
8. an item of furniture, e.g. *bookshelf, sofa*
9. an item of household equipment, e.g. *stereo system, telephone*
10. a plural noun, e.g. *children, curtains*

2. (10 points: 1 point for each appropriate answer.)
Possible Answers

1. live	6. have/eat
2. work	7. watch
3. get	8. go
4. walk	9. have/eat
5. finish	10. play

SECTION 2: GRAMMAR [30 points]

3. a. (10 points: 1 point for each correct answer.)

1. a) Her	6. c) some
2. b) in	7. b) any
3. a) a lot	8. c) watching
4. a) a	9. c) isn't
5. a) people	10. c) They're

b. (10 points: 1 point for each appropriate answer.)
Possible Answers

11. is	16. Their
12. an	17. are
13. at	18. at
14. his/the	19. very/that
15. have	20. it

4. (10 points: 1 point for each correct question.)
Possible Answers

1. How are you?
2. Where are you from?
3. What's your address?
4. What's your telephone number?
5. What's your job?/What do you do?
6. How old are you?
7. Are you married?
8. Do you have any children?
9. What color is it?
10. What time is it?/What's the time?

SECTION 3: READING [20 points]

5. (10 points: 2 points for each correct answer.)
1. Bill 2. Sally and Kate 3. Sally 4. Bill and Kate
5. Sally

6. (10 points: 2 points for each correct answer.)
1. (She watches TV) in their bedroom.
2. (She goes to a club) on the weekend.
3. (She gets some Chinese food because) she doesn't like cooking.
4. He plays football (on the weekend).
5. (She goes to movies) with her husband, Bill.

SECTION 4: WRITING [20 points]

7. (20 points)
Tell students what you will take into consideration when grading their written work. Criteria should include:
* efficient communication of meaning (7 points)
* grammatical accuracy (7 points)
* coherence in the ordering or the information or ideas (3 points)
* layout, capitalization, and punctuation (3 points)

It is probably better not to use a rigid grading system with the written part of the test. If, for example, you always deduct a point for a grammatical mistake, you may find that you are over-penalizing students who write a lot or who take risks. Deduct points if students haven't written the minimum number of sentences stated in the test.

Answers Progress Test 2 Lessons 11–20

SECTION 1: VOCABULARY [30 points]

1. a. (10 points: 1 point for each correct answer.)
1. after
2. transportation
3. ferry
4. station
5. coast
6. city
7. favorite
8. oil
9. hair
10. knit

b. (10 points: 1 point for each appropriate answer.)
1. an adverb of frequency, e.g. *often, sometimes*
2. a means of transportation, e.g. *bicycle, car*
3. an adjective, e.g. *slow, expensive*
4. a shop, e.g. *bakery, flower shop*
5. a point on the compass, e.g. *east*
6. an adjective, e.g. *lovely, modern*
7. an adjective of character, e.g. *friendly, lazy*
8. a drink, e.g. *coke, tea*
9. an adjective for describing hair, e.g. *short, straight*
10. a verb of motion, e.g. *walk*

2. (10 points: 1 point for each appropriate answer.)
1. drive
2. do
3. speak
4. buy/get
5. cook/make
6. see
7. ride
8. borrow
9. play
10. use

SECTION 2: GRAMMAR [30 points]

3. a. (10 points: 1 point for each correct answer.)
1. c) They're
2. c) of
3. c) staying
4. b) across from
5. c) was
6. b) go
7. a) visited
8. b) Are
9. c) wonderful
10. a) by

b. (10 points: 1 point for each appropriate answer.)
Possible Answers
11. do
12. have
13. some
14. How/What
15. any
16. go
17. on
18. on
19. Do
20. out

4. (10 points: 1 point for each correct question.)
Possible Answers
1. How do you go to school/work?
2. How long does it take?
3. How much is it?
4. How far is it?
5. How tall is he?
6. How old are you?
7. What's he like?
8. What does he look like?
9. What time do you get up?
10. Can you knit?

SECTION 3: READING [20 points]

5. (10 points: 2 points for each correct answer.)
1. a shower
2. coffee
3. lunch
4. dinner
5. to sleep

6. (10 points: 2 points for each correct answer.)
1. DS 2. T 3. T 4. T 5. F

SECTION 4: WRITING [20 points]

7. (20 points)
Tell students what you will take into consideration when grading their written work. Criteria should include:
* efficient communication of meaning (7 points)
* grammatical accuracy (7 points)
* coherence in the ordering or the information or ideas (3 points)
* layout, capitalization, and punctuation (3 points)

It is probably better not to use a rigid grading system with the written part of the test. If, for example, you always deduct a point for a grammatical mistake, you may find that you are over-penalizing students who write a lot or who take risks. Deduct points if students haven't written the minimum number of sentences stated in the test.

Answer Key

Lesson 1

VOCABULARY
1. Rome, Italy; Rio de Janeiro, Brazil; Washington D.C., the United States of America; Moscow, Russia; Sydney, Australia; Seoul, Korea
2. *Across:* Spain India Argentina Turkey Canada Brazil
Down: Peru Japan Greece France China Italy Russia Korea Britain Mexico Thailand
3. 1. New Delhi is in India. 2. Buenos Aires is in Argentina. 3. Paris is in France. 4.. Tokyo is in Japan. 5.. Montreal is in Canada. 6. Lima is in Peru.

FUNCTIONS
1. 1. What is your name? 2. Where are you from? 3. My name is Charlie. 4. I am from Canada. 5. Is your name Maria?
2. 1. b 2. c 5. a
4. *Verbs:* is am are be
Subject pronouns: you I

READING AND WRITING
1. **A** Hello, I'm Juan.
B Hello, Juan. My name's Anna. I'm from the Philippines. Where are you from, Juan?
A I'm from Venezuela.
2. C, B, D, A
3. *Conversation 1:* A
Conversation 2: C

Lesson 2

VOCABULARY
1. *Jobs:* teacher waiter receptionist doctor chef actor artist police officer nurse journalist farmer
2. 1. He's a waiter. 2. She's an artist. 3. He's a chef. 4. She's a doctor. 5. He's a farmer. 6. They're police officers.
3. 1. her 2. Moscow 3. we 4. Brazil 5. friend 6. your
5. 1. from 2. student 3. Canada 4. friend 5. English

GRAMMAR
1. 1. They're 2. You're 3. Their 4. your 5. Their
2. 1. He's 2. His 3. He's 4. his 5. He's
3. 1. She's a secretary. 2. They're from Australia. 3. He's an actor. 4. They're doctors. 5. We're farmers.
4. 1. He is 2. They are 3. I am 4. We are 5. They are 6. She is

READING
1. 1. Maria is a receptionist.

2. Jim is a jazz musician.
3. Kathy is an economist.
4. Hiroshi is a journalist.
5. Emma is a nurse.
2. 1. No, he is from Japan.
2. No, she is from Mexico City.
3. No, she is a nurse.
4. No, he is a jazz musician.
5. No, they are teachers.
3. His name is Hiroshi. He's from Japan. He's a journalist for an international magazine. His wife's name is Kathy and she's from Chicago. She's an economist.

Lesson 3

VOCABULARY
1. *Nouns:* student children Japan doctor last name phone number brother actor friend address first name job boyfriend
Adjectives: married single good-looking

GRAMMAR
1. 1. c 2. d 3. e 4. a 5. f 6. b
2. 1. Where 2. How 3. What 4. Who 5. Where 6. What
4. *Possible Answers*
1. Is she married? 2. Are you single? 3. Are his children students? 4. Is he from Detroit? 5. Are you an economist? 6. Is she a teacher?
5. 1. No, she isn't. She's from Chile. 2. No, he isn't. He's a nurse. 3. No, they aren't. They're Argentinian. 4. No, she isn't. She's seventeen. 5. No, he isn't. He's married.

READING
1. an interview for an apartment
2. What's your name? What's your job? How old are you? Are you American?
3. 2. What's her name?
3. How old is she?
4. Is she American?
4. 1. She's a receptionist.
2. Her name is Maria Verde
3. She's twenty-five years old.
4. She's Mexican.

WRITING
1. Picture A: Janvi Singh
Picture C: May Downs
Picture D: Michael Haines

Lesson 4

VOCABULARY
1. 1: one 2: two 8: eight 11:eleven 12: twelve 13: thirteen 15: fifteen 17: seventeen 20: twenty 33: thirty-three 47: forty-seven 96: ninety-six
2. 1. room 2. chair 3. interesting 4. that
4. 1. kind/good 2. good/kind 3. interesting 4. comfortable 5. beautiful

GRAMMAR
1. classrooms teachers addresses

numbers colleges classes chairs
2. 1. There is 2. There are 3. There is 4. There are 5. There is
3. 1. It's a very interesting lesson. 2. They're very comfortable chairs.
3. It's an international class.
4. She's a very popular teacher.
5. San Francisco is a very beautiful city.
6. They're very kind people.

READING
1. It is a bilingual school.
2. new bilingual old modern big friendly big comfortable big special small good expensive
3. 1. No, it isn't. 2. It's for children. 3. They are six and nine years old. 4. It's downtown. 5. It's an old building but inside it's modern.

Lesson 5

VOCABULARY
1. *Electronic products:* calculator camera computer cellular phone walkman radio
Office things: calculator computer calendar notebook pen pencil
Jobs: accountant doctor farmer vet
Places: city country library school
2. A. keys B. calendar C. comb D. calculator E. glasses F. credit card G. gloves H. brush I. watch J. camera
3. A. near B. in C. under D. on
4. 1. How 2. What 3. What 4. Where
5. 1. blue 2. brown 3. orange 4. pink 5. red 6. purple 7. black 8. gray 9. white 10. green 11. yellow

GRAMMAR
1. 1. I am a teacher from Colombia. 2. You are an English student.
3. She is a manager at a bank.
4. They are my keys, not yours.
5. It is on the table.
6. He is twenty-five years old today.

READING
2. *Possible Answer*
There is one chair in the room. The computer is on the table. The desk is in the middle of the room. On the desk there is a telephone and a lamp. My books are on the table. There's a pen on the floor under the desk. There's a painting on the wall near my desk.

Lesson 6

VOCABULARY
1.

Male	**Female**
man	woman
boy	girl
father	mother
brother	sister

nephew   niece
son   daughter
husband   wife
uncle   aunt
grandfather   grandmother
cousin   cousin
2. 1. aunt 2. niece 3. grandmother 4. son 5. brother 6. cousin
3. men women children families people wives countries

READING AND GRAMMAR
2. *Family A:* Jenny is thirty-two years old and has got a job in a post office in a small town. She's divorced and has an eight-year-old daughter, Cindy, and a three-year-old son, Jamie. She has a small house with a big yard in the town. She has a lot of friends in the town. Jenny's mother, Kate, lives in the same town. She helps Jenny with the children when she's at work.
Family B: Peter is thirty-nine years old and he is an architect in Denver. He is married to Elizabeth and they have four children: three sons and a daughter. They live in a big house near Denver. Elizabeth takes care of the children and has a part-time job at a school near her home. Peter's parents, Kathleen and Mike, live in the country and come to stay with the family during vacations. They have a comfortable life and they are a happy family.
3. 1. Jenny is divorced. (Elizabeth's husband is Peter.) 2. Elizabeth has a part-time job in a school. (Peter is an architect.) 3. Peter has four children. (Jenny has two children.) 4. Jenny has a job in a post office. (Elizabeth has a part-time job in a school.) 5. Jenny has a house in a town. (Peter and Elizabeth have a house near Denver.)
4. 1. Elizabeth is Peter's wife.
2. Kathleen and Mike are Peter's parents.
3. Cindy is Jenny's daughter/ Kate's granddaughter/ Jamie's sister.
4. Jamie is Jenny's son/Kate's grandson/Cindy's brother.
6. *Passage 1:* Vivienne
Passage 2: Eddy
7. 1. teacher 2. British 3. computer 4. married

Lesson 7

VOCABULARY
1. 1. It's twenty past four in the afternoon.
2. It's a quarter to eleven in the morning.
3. It's nine o'clock in the evening.

74

4. It's eleven thirty in the morning.
   5. It's a quarter past six in the morning.
2. 1. get up 2. have breakfast
   3. start work 4. have lunch
   5. finish work 6. have dinner
   7. go to bed

GRAMMAR
1. 1. in   2. at   3. on   4. in
   5. on   6. at
4. 1. We don't go to bed at midnight.
   2. My children don't get up at eight.
   3. I don't have lunch in a restaurant.
   4. Most people don't work on the weekend.
   5. We don't go shopping on Saturday mornings.

READING
1. A: start finish starts finishes
   work don't go go have
   have go have
3. 1. (✗) 2. (✗) 3. (✓) 4. (✓)(✗)
   5. (✓) 6. (✓)(✗) 7. (✗) 8. (✓)

Lesson 8
GRAMMAR AND READING
1. 1. are 2. is   3. are 4. aren't
   5. Are 6. isn't 7. Is   8. is
2. 1. any 2. some 3. some
   4. any 5. any   6. some
3. *Room A:* study
   Room B: living room
4. 1. study 2. upstairs, bathroom
   3. bookshelves 4. window, computer 5. mirror, armchair

WRITING AND READING
2. Japan
3. 1. F 2. T 3. F 4. F 5. T

Lesson 9
VOCABULARY
1. *Across:* relax live watch get drink make play do go eat sing
   Down: read study wash work take see come like start finish
2. 1. take 2. watch 3. make 4. eat, drink 5. play 6. study
3. 1. f 2. a 3. e 4. b 5. g 6. d 7. h 8. c

GRAMMAR
1. 1. He/She takes a sauna on Wednesday evenings. 2. He/She watches sports on TV on Monday night. 3. He/She makes Sunday dinner for the family. 4. He/She eats a sandwich and drinks mineral water for lunch. 5. He/She plays guitar in a rock band with friends. 6. He/She studies Spanish at evening classes.
2. 1. Where 2. How 3. Who 4. What 5. When

READING
1. a man
2. He makes dinner. He watches sports on TV. He goes running. He reads. He watches television.
3. She goes to language classes. She goes to a friend's house for dinner. She works on her computer.
4. They have a drink. They sit and have dinner and watch TV. They go to the movies. They have a drink at a bar. They get up at noon. They go to the supermarket. They go to a restaurant or to a nightclub. They go to her parents' house.
5. *Passage A:* a schoolchild
   Passage B: a mother
   Passage C: a business person
6. *Passage A:* After school. He plays soccer and basketball with his friends.
   Passage B: At eight o'clock. She has a cup of coffee and reads the newspaper.
   Passage C: At twelve thirty. He/She gets a sandwich and goes for a long walk in the park.

Lesson 10
VOCABULARY
1. *Possible Answers*
   play: sports, football, baseball, tennis, guitar, piano
   watch: TV, sports, a football game listen to: the radio, music, a concert

GRAMMAR
1.

Subject	Object
I	me
you	you
he	him
she	her
it	it
we	us
they	them

2. 1. it 2. them 3. it 4. her 5. them 6. him
3. 1. Do you like classical music?
   2. What is your favorite music?
   3. I don't like skiing at all.
   4. Do you like watching movies?
   5. I don't like it very much.
4. 1. I like eating Chinese food.
   2. I like watching TV.
   3. I like going to the movies.
   4. I like playing computer games.
   5. I like drinking tea.

READING
1. 1. c 2. d 3. e 4. a 5. b
2. 1. American 2. Philadelphia 3. Ecuadorian 4. Quito
3. He likes basketball, football, going to see big games, going to the movies, and (jazz) music.

Lesson 11
VOCABULARY AND GRAMMAR
1. late punctual early on time
6. 1. get up 2. take 3. have 4. leaves 5. read 6. leave 7. have 8. works 9. get 10. go 11. get 12. have
7. *Possible Answers*
   taxi driver: car city streets map nightwork drive
   teacher: classroom pupils school desk folder teach
   chef: food restaurant dinner cook lunch
   musician: dancing club guitar rock concert play
9. *Possible Answers*
   1. teacher 2. musician 3. chef 4. taxi driver

READING AND SPEAKING
1. *Taxi driver:* Sentences 8 and 10
   Teacher: Sentences 3, 7, and 9
   Chef: Sentences 2 and 5
   Musician: Sentences 1, 4, 6, 11, and 12
3. musician
4. 1. 11 2. 1 3. 6 4. 12

Lesson 12
VOCABULARY
Possible Answers
Picture A: by bus, crowded, slow, cheap, dangerous, hot, uncomfortable
Picture B: by plane, expensive, fast, fly
Picture C: by bicycle, cheap, crowded

READING
1. Picture A
2. many journeys take a day; there is a bus only once or twice a week; dangerous; break down; roads in bad condition; very slow and uncomfortable; very crowded
3. It is cheap.

GRAMMAR
1. 1. a bus – buses
   2. a subway – subways
   3. a ferry – ferries
   4. an airport – airports
   5. a house – houses
   6. an office – offices
   7. a delay – delays
   8. an hour – hours
2. 1. The, the 2. – 3. a 4. – 5. a 6. the 7. a, a 8. The 9. – 10. the, –
3. a. 3 b. 5 c. 8 d. 6 e. 1 f. 9 g. 2 h. 10 i. 7 j. 4
4. *Possible Answers*
   1. How long does it take?
   2. How do you get to work?
   3. Do you go very often?
   4. How much is it?
   5. How far is it?

Lesson 13
VOCABULARY AND GRAMMAR
1. *Across:* 3. swim 6. cook 8. drink 9. be 12. do 13. ride 17. read 18. win 19. fly
   Down: 1. ski 2. hold 4. walk 5. meet 7. knit 10. go 1.1 drive 14. draw 15. eat 16. play 17. run
2. 1. ride 2. fly 3. read 4. play 5. eat 6. run/ski
4. 1. can't 2. can't 3. can, can't 4. can 5. can, can't
5. 1. d 2. a 3. e 4. c 5. b
7. *Possible Answers*
   1. Can you swim/play guitar?
   2. I can't cook.
   3. Can you ski/play piano?
   4. I can speak Spanish.

READING AND WRITING
1. A. camera B. bed C. TV D. dishwasher E. mirror F. fireplace
2. 1. dishwasher 2. bed 3. TV 4. camera 5. fireplace 6. mirror
3. is wash sleep lie put on watch use take carry sit look see
4. 1. It is usually in the kitchen.
   2. It is often upstairs in a house.
   3. This is often in the living room.
   4. ...you can carry it in your bag.
   5. It is often in the living room.
   6. It can be on a wall in any room in the house. There is always one in the bathroom.

Lesson 14
VOCABULARY
1. send eat take out change buy
2. *Post office:* stamps send buy letters envelopes
   Music store: buy cassette CDs
   Drugstore: sunscreen medicine buy aspirin
   Bank: account money traveler's checks take out change
   Station: buy platform ticket train
   Restaurant: meal eat menu buy dinner

GRAMMAR AND READING
2. on the eastern side; in; on the other side of; across from; near; on the corner of; on
3. 1. department store 2. bookstore 3. bus station 4. park 5. library 6. farmers' market 7. city hall 8. opera house 9. cathedral
4. 1. across from 2. between 3. near 4. on the corner of 5. near/across from 6. near

FUNCTIONS AND READING
1. *Conversation 1:* bookstore
   Conversation 2: library
2. *Possible Answer*
   Walk along Post Street. Turn left on Riverside. The music store is after the parking lot.
3. *Possible Answer*
   Walk along Washington Street. Turn left on Spokane Falls

Boulevard. Turn right and walk through the park. The farmer's market is across from the Spokane Arena.

WRITING
1. Where can I buy some vegetables? Is it far? Can you tell me where it is, please? And where re the vegetable stalls? Is there a flower shop? Thank you.

Lesson 15

GRAMMAR
1. enjoying staying passing having living learning shopping sitting flying traveling taking lying writing
2. 1. are staying 2. is lying 3. are having 4. are flying 5. are enjoying
4. *Possible answers*
   2. What are you doing tonight?
   3. Who are you going with?
   4. Are you enjoying the movie?
   5. What are you learning at evening class?

VOCABULARY
1. beautiful – ugly; east – west; interesting – boring; old-fashioned – modern; north – south; cold – hot; dark – light; quiet – noisy
2. *Picture A:* sea coast port
   Picture B: skiing mountains snow cold holiday
   Picture C: modern industrial town river
3. *Possible Answers*
   Picture A: lively interesting
   Picture B: beautiful
   Picture C: ugly
4. Picture B
5. I'm having   I'm learning
   I'm enjoying   I'm staying

READING AND WRITING
1. It is in the south of California on the coast. It is between the sea and the hills.
2. beautiful location   pleasant climate   surfing   diving fishing   art festivals   romance restaurants   sunsets

Lesson 16

VOCABULARY AND READING
1. 1. d 2. a 3. c 4. b
2. *dog:* noisy   not obedient
   girlfriend: shy   cute
   girlfriend's hair: dark
   vacation in Hawaii: exciting wonderful   hot (weather)
   cabin vacation: terrible horrible (weather)
   children: not well-behaved
   parents: bad-tempered
   caravan holiday: terrible

GRAMMAR
1. 1. was 2. were 3. was 4. were 5. were 6. was
2. 1. Where were you born?
   2. What were you like at school?
   3. What were you good at?
   4. Were you often in trouble in school?

READING AND WRITING
1. 1. b 2. a 3. f 4. c 5. e 6. d

Lesson 17

VOCABULARY
1. 1. rice 2. bacon 3. potato 4. oil 5. salt 6. onion

READING AND WRITING
1. 1. true 2. false 3. false 4. false 5. true 6. true 7. true 8. false
2. *common:* chopsticks with the Chinese population; smoking
   crowded, noisy and hot: restaurants in the early evening
   relaxed: restaurants
3. *C:* table meal spoon fingers restaurants
   U: food salt fish sauce alcohol drink
4. 2. Only the Chinese population use chopsticks.
   3. They use their fingers.
   4. They can drink alcohol.
   8. Restaurants are very relaxed.

GRAMMAR
1. *U:* wine oil yoghurt butter pork milk water beef bread tea salt rice soup pasta cheese
   C: apple egg onion lemon carrot steak
2. 1. some 2. some 3. a 4. any 5. some 6. a
3. at a restaurant
4. 1. some 2. any 3. some 4. a 5. any 6. a 7. any 8. some 9. any 10. some 11. some 12. any

Lesson 18

VOCABULARY
2. 1. hit 2. teenager 3. album 4. musician 5. band 6. award 7. guitar
3. 1. g 2. d 3. a 4. f 5. c 6. h 7. e 8. b

GRAMMAR AND READING
1. appeared received died learned lived composed married moved played started worked finished
2. 1. married 2. appeared 3. learned 4. worked 5. received 6. started
3. Maria Callas was one of the greatest soprano singers of this century. She was born in 1923 in New York to Greek parents. She moved to Greece and studied singing at the Athens

Conservatoire. She first appeared in the opera in Athens. In 1945 she moved to Italy and worked at La Scala in Milan. She died in 1977.
4. 1. soprano singer 2. New York 3. Athens 4. Athens/Italy/ La Scala 5. 1977
5. studied went appeared directed received appeared was didn't receive directed appeared was
6. 1. He studied business at the University of California.
   2. He directed his first film in 1982./He appeared in his first film in 1981.
   3. He received an Oscar in 1990 for *Dances with Wolves*.
   4. His most expensive film was *Waterworld*.
7. 1. learned 2. started 3. played/ appeared 4. lived 5. moved/ went 6. moved 7. married 8. worked 9. composed/ wrote 10. died

Lesson 19

VOCABULARY
2. *Possible Answers*
   Picture A: The woman isn't thin. She has straight hair. She doesn't have glasses.
   Picture B: The man is young and thin. He has fair hair.
   Picture C: The woman is young/middle-aged. She has dark straight hair. She is tall.

FUNCTIONS
1. *Possible Answers*
   1. What's he like?
   2. What does she look like?
   3. How tall is she?
   4. How old is he?
   5. Who does she look like?

READING
1. 1. a lost child 2. a criminal
2. 1. He has short, dark hair.
   2. He's wearing a blue sweater, yellow shorts, and white sneakers.
   3. He's at the information desk.
3. 1. dangerous 2. twenty-five 3. medium- 4. short, blond, moustache 5. jeans, sweater, black

Lesson 20

VOCABULARY
1. *Across:* did made bought took said lost went spent became
   Down: found had gave got came wrote
2. 1. wrote 2. went 3. did 4. took 5. made 6. lost
3. 1. b 2. e 3. f 4. a 5. c 6. d

GRAMMAR
1. 1. Did you visit a museum yesterday?
   2. Did you write some postcards on the weekend?
   3. Did you go shopping yesterday?
   4. Did you go to a restaurant on Saturday?
   5. Did you take a train last week?
3. *Possible Answers*
   1. Did you stay at home last night?
   2. Did you go to the movies yesterday?
   3. Did you go shopping?
   4. Did he go on vacation?

READING
1. 1. Diana. 2. She is writing to Bob. 3. No, she is travelling with Mike.
2. 1. It was sunny and warm.
   2. She spent four days in New York.
   3. She flew to Chicago.
   4. She had some wonderful food in small restaurants.
   5. She lost her purse on the L-train.
   6. She went to Los Angeles after Chicago.
   7. She stayed in a hotel.
   8. She spent two days by the sea.